THE DEAFENING SOUND OF SORROW

Kerrie Ann Brown Left a Beautiful Memory

KATHLEEN RICARD

Black Rose Writing | Texas

©2025 by Kathleen Ricard
All rights reserved. No part of this book may be reproduced, stored in a retrieval system or transmitted in any form or by any means without the prior written permission of the publishers, except by a reviewer who may quote brief passages in a review to be printed in a newspaper, magazine or journal.

The author grants the final approval for this literary material.

First printing

This is a work of fiction. Names, characters, businesses, places, events, and incidents are either the products of the author's imagination or used in a fictitious manner. Any resemblance to actual persons, living or dead, or actual events is purely coincidental.

ISBN: 978-1-68513-662-8
LIBRARY OF CONGRESS CONTROL NUMBER: 2025936198
PUBLISHED BY BLACK ROSE WRITING
www.blackrosewriting.com

Printed in the United States of America
Suggested Retail Price (SRP) $18.95

The Deafening Sound of Sorrow is printed in Garamond Premier Pro

*As a planet-friendly publisher, Black Rose Writing does its best to eliminate unnecessary waste to reduce paper usage and energy costs, while never compromising the reading experience. As a result, the final word count vs. page count may not meet common expectations.

PRAISE FOR
THE DEAFENING SOUND OF SORROW

"Utterly captivating, a poignant, heart-wrenching true account of a horrible crime and its effects on those left behind. Rife with raw honesty yet beautifully told."
—Mary Ellen Bramwell, award-winning author of *When I Was Seven*

"How does one write about a forty-year-old cold case? Kathleen Ricard does so heartbreakingly in her debut memoir entitled The Deafening Sound of Sorrow, recounting how Kerrie Ann Brown's brutal murder in Thompson, Manitoba forever altered the lives of her friends. With resilience and compassion beyond their years, they supported one another while finding a way to honour Kerrie's memory. *The Deafening Sound of Sorrow* is not simply an account of a cold case. It's a cautionary tale, a lesson in courage, and a testament to a young girl who left a lasting impression on everyone she met."
—Maureen Ulrich, author of the *Winds of Change* series

This book is dedicated to the youth of Thompson, Manitoba, who will forever symbolize hope for a better tomorrow.

THE DEAFENING SOUND OF SORROW

"...our memories are basically myths and you think about them so many times and nobody remembers. We remember remembering. You know, that's what it is." —Shawn Simmons, during an interview on CBC's "Somebody Knows Something" with host David Ridgen, October, 2021.

PROLOGUE
IN THE END...

Immediately following the brutal rape and murder of Kerrie Ann Brown on October 16th, 1986, a tidal wave of disbelief, shock, and grief crashed down on Thompson, Manitoba, leaving behind a residue of fear that it could happen again. But it didn't happen again. And with each passing year that Kerrie's murder remains unsolved, the hope for justice fades away, much like the cool gray ashes of a smoldering campfire floating aimlessly up into the Manitoba sky, scattered by those unforgiving northern winds.

When the memory of my young friend resurfaces, it is usually on the anniversary of her death or a significant life event that, because of her, is a sharp reminder to count my life's blessings. These milestones also serve as a painful reminder of the intricate value of the life that was taken from the fifteen-year-old girl so many years ago. Even after all these years, I can still picture her slightly crooked smile, her pale porcelain, doll-like features surrounded by her blonde curly hair, highlighted by her easy-going, infectious personality. Shortly after these moments of reminiscences with Kerrie, a bitter taste of seasoned hatred would implode in my mouth, forcing me to also remember the monsters who took her life and who have seemingly gotten away with it. Never have I ever hated with so much intensity and longevity that, at times, has made me physically ill. Kerrie's killers may never be caught, a harsh truth that has made me wonder in recent years, "What the fuck was the point of Kerrie's short life and brutal, violent death?" That question, along with my vibrating cell phone in the back pocket of my jeans, would become the driving force behind me writing this book almost four decades later.

On the eve of the thirty-fifth anniversary of Kerrie's murder, I answered my iPhone from an unknown caller and was surprised to hear, "Hi, Kat!" blasting in my ear. No one had called me by my childhood nickname for a very long time. I did, however, instantly recognize the male voice from my teenage past.

Chris Jones and I quickly calculated it had been thirty years since we had last spoken. Not long into our catch-up conversation, I sadly learned he had lived most of those thirty years battling addiction. I sat on my couch and listened in sober silence as he told me his life story, describing the different drugs he had been addicted to between his many rehab stints. I tried to picture what he looked like now, a fifty-something year old recovering drug addict, but could only conjure up the brown-haired, brown-eyed, funny, witty, full-of-life teenage boy he had once been. With a slight slur in his speech, Chris assured me he was now committed to his sobriety, pausing occasionally to take a drag or sip off something.

Inevitably, our conversation turned to our shared childhood friend and the status of her murder case. As I sipped my lukewarm tea, I noticed with the change in subject, the tone of his voice had also changed. He sounded more animated as he spoke about the podcast *Someone Knows Something* by the Canadian Broadcasting Company (CBC). David Ridgen, a true crime reporter, recently re-reported the details of Kerrie's case, hoping to spark new information in what the Royal Canadian Mounted Police (RCMP) was now referring to as "one of Manitoba's coldest murder cases." Chris became overly enthusiastic when he told me about a new genealogical DNA test that was showing promising results in the United States in solving cold cases. His tone revealed his intense desire in wanting—no, scratch that—*needing* to know who had brutally taken our friend's life over three decades ago. It was as if his own life depended on it. An image of him began to materialize, and who I saw made me angry. He was stuck. Stuck in his hatred for the monsters who took our friend's life. Stuck in his pain, sorrow, and grief, but more importantly, he was stuck back in 1986. Kerrie would not have wanted that for him or for anyone else who mourned her. I bit my bottom lip, finding myself once again internally raging at Kerrie's killers, who had apparently destroyed yet another innocent life. Her legacy was so much more than those who had murdered her.

It was no different from those crosses or flowers people placed along the side of highways to mark the spot where their loved one had died, obviously in a car accident. Beyond being a safety issue or distraction to drivers, I often wondered what was the point of memorializing the spot where someone had died? Or how they died? Wouldn't marking their favourite or most loved place on earth when they were living make more sense? I sat quietly, stewing while Chris carried on the conversation without me.

"Hey, where is the book you wrote about Kerrie?" he asked.

I was surprised by his question, and took a deep breath as my mind flashed to the banker box safely tucked away in the back of my walk-in closet. Of course, he knew about the book I had written so long ago because anyone who knew me, back then and now, knew I was a writer. So, this was the reason for his out-of-the-blue phone call. "It's not finished," I confessed.

"Why not?"

I wracked my brain, trying to remember why I hadn't finished the book. I also felt guilty for not thinking about the manuscript in years. "I guess because there's no ending. Because no one has ever been convicted of her murder?" Without meaning to, my answers came out as questions.

This set him off again, listing possible suspects and thanking God that with this new DNA test, we had a good chance of finding the murderers.

"Does it matter who killed Kerrie?" I cut him off mid-sentence. I was sorry, but not sorry for interrupting him. I was losing patience with the subject of who-done-it, which kept us on a never-ending conversation loop. Also, I couldn't help but think, albeit harshly, that if he had put this much passion into his own choices, then maybe his life would have turned out differently. I knew I was being unfairly judgemental as I could only go so far in imagining his shoe size then trying to walk in them, but I couldn't help but feel as if I was mourning yet another childhood friend—the teenage boy he once was.

"What do you mean?" he asked. "You *don't* care who killed Kerrie?"

"It's not that I don't care. I do. What I'm trying to say is, what difference would it make today if we found out who killed Kerrie thirty-five years ago?"

"I don't understand. . ." His voice trailed off.

"Just hear me out." I felt a sudden urge to stand up and pace my living room, like I was in front of a jury. "Close your eyes and pick someone. Anyone. Choose the monster or monsters who killed Kerrie or took part in killing her. Would knowing who they are make any difference in your life today? In my life? Would it change what happened to her? It wouldn't bring her back. And, if you could ask them why they did it? Is there any answer they could give you that would bring you peace or justify what they did to her?" I stopped to take a deep breath. "So, in the end, my dear friend, does it really matter who killed Kerrie?"

I plopped back down on the couch, pulled my knees up to my chest, bit down on my bottom lip, and waited. After a minute that felt more like five, I pulled the phone away from my ear to glance down at the screen, convinced Chris had hung up on me. To my surprise, the line was still alive and approaching the one-hour mark.

"I don't know." His voice had lost its oomph. "But I do know Kerrie deserves justice, and that means finding whoever killed her. So, yes, it does matter who did it." His voice gained momentum. "As for bringing me peace, I'll let you know once the monsters are caught. Either way, you need to finish her book."

"How?" I snapped. "Ironically, without knowing who killed Kerrie, her book has no ending."

He took a long drag off something and exhaled loudly in my ear. "I have faith that you, my old friend, will figure it out. Because in the end. . .no one else can write our story but you."

Easier said than done, I thought.

***

For days after that phone call, that one sentence replayed in my head over and over—no one else could write our story. Our story? What exactly was our story?

A week later, I found myself sitting cross-legged on the floor of my walk-in closet, taking the lid off that old banker's box to carefully place the memories of 1986 on the carpet around me. I pulled out old newspaper clippings covered in protective plastic, letters to the editor I had written to the local newspapers long ago, my journals, character sketches, the book's outline, and a stack of pictures.

Flipping through the old photos a sudden powerful wave of nostalgia washed over me as I sat in the shallow pool of my past. I traced one fingertip over the young, laughing faces of all my friends from so long ago. I stopped to study one poorly developed photo in particular that was taken in the basement on Trout Ave. My heart skipped that old familiar beat when I saw my old boyfriend smiling back at me, phone in hand, holding up a bottle of whiskey as if to toast the camera. Our friends sat on the couch in front of him, all of them grinning, their faces slightly out of focus. I was sure the picture had captured a moment before Kerrie's murder, during a time when life was as it should be for any teenager—happy and carefree.

When my fingernails scratched the surface of the manuscript, I lifted it from the depths of the box and stretched my stiff legs out in front of me to place the yellow-tinted typewritten pages on my lap. It took some effort to coax the stiff black clip off the corner. After reading the first few pages, I had to force myself to continue. While skimming the rest of the book, I couldn't help but groan out loud at the grammatical errors and shake my head at the poorly structured sentences, mentally scolding myself. After force reading the last page, I shuffled the pages together loosely, reattached the black clip, and tossed it back into the box. The writing was awful. The plot was weak, the characters one dimensional, and the theme pointed in one direction only: who killed Kerrie Ann Brown? I rubbed my face with both hands hard, trying to erase the overpowering feeling of dread, an emotional reminder of why I had stopped writing the book in the first place. And like I had explained to Chris, the book had no ending because whoever killed Kerrie was still out there.

As I gathered the remains of 1986 to put them back in the box, I realized, sadly, that Kerrie would most likely always be remembered as one of the "coldest murder cases in Manitoba's history", which felt so wrong to me.

Kerrie had been a cute, ordinary, lovable, fun teenage girl. Before her murder, I treasured the memories of all of us just hanging out together—

partying, cruising the city streets, playing car tag or car surfing, shooting pool at the Thompson Billiards, eating fries with gravy at Chicken Chef, or playing cards games in the forum at school. After her murder, the bond of the many friendships Kerrie left behind grew stronger as we forged ahead, together, determined to do something positive in the aftermath of her tragic death—like raising ten thousand dollars for her scholarship fund and creating the streetwise group Youth for a Better Tomorrow. Who could forget picking those damn purple pinecones in subzero temperatures in the bush during the winter of '87 for Manitoba Forestry (Manfor), all to raise money for Kerrie's scholarship fund? This memory hit me particularly hard, bringing up those old tears from so long ago. I quickly blinked them away as I secured the lid on the box and slapped it shut with both hands. When it hit me—there may never be an ending to Kerrie's story. The finality of that thought both unsettled and calmed me at the same time. Maybe whoever killed Kerrie was better left to the unknown because, like I had said to Chris, did it really matter who killed Kerrie after all these years? I wondered as I pushed 1986 back into the depths of my closet. I knew one thing for sure—I did not want to be sucked back down into that emotional black hole filled with the horrific details of her rape and violent death, which would eventually smother me with that dark cloud of profound sadness.

Today, I wanted to remember Kerrie for who she was, the good times we had and the friends we shared, and focus on what she taught me in the short time I knew her, which, I would forever be grateful for.

Maybe that was our story?

I stood up slowly, giving my forty-nine-year-old knees the time they needed to adjust to my new position, as the idea of *our story* began to unfold in my head before going to find my laptop.

CHAPTER 1
ONLY THE MONSTERS WOULD KNOW

The following is based on actual events and contains descriptions of violence that may be disturbing to some readers. Reader discretion is advised.

The names of some characters have been changed to protect their identities.

Thursday, October 16th, 1986, at approximately 11:30 p.m.

Kerrie stepped out into the fresh October night air, letting the backdoor slam shut behind her, which muffled the sounds of teenage laughter mixed with the Eagle's band singing "Hotel California." She flipped her short, curly blonde hair, which framed her pale white features, over the collar of her favourite black and gold Pittsburgh Penguins jacket, that hung loose on her slim frame. She reeked of cigarette smoke, proof of her having spent the last few hours surrounded by all her friends in the dimly lit basement on Trout Ave. At fifteen years old, Kerrie did not smoke.

Despite the apparent contradiction in their appearances, Kerrie and Natalie had always been best friends. Where Kerrie was petite, fair-skinned, and shy, Natalie was tall, dark, and bold. Both girls had been drinking that night. Natalie more so than Kerrie, which was evident in her glassy brown eyes and giddiness when they reached the small landing at the top of the stairs. As they balanced on a pile of shoes, Natalie realized she had forgotten her purse and told Kerrie to "stay put" before going back down the stairs to get it.

Kerrie wanted to leave the party the minute Chad showed up with a new girl on his arm. Even though it had not gotten serious between them in the short period that they had dated, Kerrie had to leave just the same. Against her best friend's orders, Kerrie left, to walk across the blanket of pure white snow that covered the pathway from the back door of the plain square white house with the brown trim down the sloped driveway. Her sneakers disappeared briefly in the fluffy white powder, leaving a trail of size-five footprints that abruptly ended on the snow-covered seam that separated the darkened driveway from the well-lit street.

Kerrie's outfit—black leggings splashed with a pink leopard print pattern that matched her pink T-shirt—was chosen specifically for the party and not for the long cold walk home, which was clear across town. She had previously promised to sleep at Natalie's house that night, just two streets over from where she would vanish.

Whether Kerrie went willingly or was taken is not known and is of little significance. What is known is that within the confines of her abduction, she tried to fight back. Her wounds would later corroborate her courageous efforts to defend herself. But even with adrenaline-infused blood pumping through her veins, she would succumb to her captors, as she was outnumbered and outweighed.

Kerrie was forced to travel along the snow-covered streets as the vehicle maneuvered cautiously over a deep dip in the road while steering the curves of Westwood Drive. At the intersection on Thompson Drive, the turn signal blinked to indicate north towards the outskirts of town. The bright streetlamps lining Thompson Drive may have cast flashes of light within the vehicle, briefly illuminating the faces of her abductors.

Kerrie may have felt and heard the sudden thump the tires made when driven over the start line of the Burntwood Bridge. Within the seconds it took to cross over the steel and cement structure that stretched straight and high above the fast-moving Burntwood River, her irrational childhood fears of that bridge may have resurfaced. The water below had always been known for its perpetual rage, with its relentless rapids capped off in white that never stopped moving long enough for the freezing temperatures to catch it. Both sides of the bridge had guard rails with evenly spaced pole lamps that shot up straight and then curved, which eerily resembled that of curled fingers on outstretched hands. These clawed fingertips cast an ominous yellow glow of light that had the power to discolour any car that passed underneath.

Kerrie was taken past the popular burger joint, closed for the season, to continue on the Mystery Lake highway before sharply turning left onto a gravel road and passing an out-of-place farm where boarded horses slept. When the vehicles stopped at the road's dead end, four headlights may have shone a spotlight on a wide clearing carved into the dense forest known as a hydro line. A man-made path, twenty meters wide, cut into the bush that provided unobstructed passage for the power lines running through the northern Manitoba forest.

At fifteen years, two months, and two days, Kerrie would learn that monsters do, in fact, exist. Within the hours that followed her abduction, she endured unimaginable brutality at the hands of these monsters. Their deformed characters and shared morbid motivation led them to commit such vile acts on a defenseless teenage girl. Whether they were boys or men is of little consequence. Because of these heinous actions, it would confirm the absence of a human conscience, which would prove beyond a shadow of any doubt that monsters are monsters regardless of age.

Kerrie was made to strip vulnerable before she was forced to suffer the tortures of rape, twice. If she had pleaded for mercy, none was given. Her only protection, *with hopeful speculation,* is that within these horrific hours she covered herself with a heavy, thick blanket of shock. While under shock's protection, the essence of time would become obtuse by changing Kerrie's clarity of consciousness into a thick fog of confusion, using shock's power to turn those horrific hours into excruciating seconds that stretched into agony-filled moments. When it was over, Kerrie redressed herself in clothes that reeked of shame.

The monsters would then collect logs and rip branches from innocent bystanding spruce, pine, and aspen trees. With the murder weapons in hand, they would carry out the first act of murder, and with each strike, they solidified their homicidal pact, which would sustain their conspiracy of silence for years.

Kerrie raised her bare arms to shield herself from the feral blows at first, which left a forensic blood-splatter pattern on the surrounding foliage before she collapsed on defenseless ground.

Her unconscious body was placed face down on her favourite jacket, with one sneaker pulled off, revealing a bright white ankle-sock. The blood that gushed from her head wounds would forever change her hair colour from a white blonde to a dark red before settling on the frozen ground beneath her disfigured features. With one arm reaching above her head and the other tucked awkwardly down by her side, her bare arms were a brilliant bright white against the backdrop of the forest floor, as if purposely posed like that of a mannequin.

The deadly silence of the forest would then be interrupted by noises. A car engine revved madly, its tires spinning aimlessly, digging deeper in the mud. Vehicle doors slammed shut. Voices were raised in a panic language. With one vehicle's tires bogged down in the soft earth, a hasty plan was concocted, using materials on hand. A square black vinyl floor mat was jammed behind one tire, and a deflated red-blue air mattress, folded in half, and was placed on bloody sticks and shoved behind the other. The frustrated growls of entrapment drowned out any sounds of a badly injured girl disposed of nearby. Kerrie's bruises taking the time needed to turn into the ugliest shade of blue-black-yellow, while she laboured to breathe through a broken nose.

When the vehicle was freed, the monsters left behind a lasting impression: a partial size eight or nine footprint beside rutted tire tracks, which would only later prove their combined determination. Fuelled by self-preservation, they drove away without a second glance back at a young life's devastation.

Within the rules of life's unfairness, they continue to travel on a road paved with injustice—free from prosecution, living cloaked in lies, covered up by their collective deception, showing no signs of remorse or regret and seeking no redemption. To this very day, the monsters live, hidden, out in the open and in plain sight, wearing human disguises that have, unfairly, grown old. *How can anyone live a lifetime knowing the part they played in the taking of a young girl's life? To see the face of evil each day, while washing their blood-stained hands?* Only the monsters would know.

Kerrie was an extra-ordinary pretty-cute girl who lived fifteen years, two months, and one day. She had been blessed with two loving parents, two annoying brothers, and two best friends, who, for a time, lived within pajama-walking distance. She lived a simple teenager's life—going to school and spending all her free time with her many friends. She was an average student with her favourite best subject being English. Kerrie was as happy as any teenage girl could be, with a young heart filled with dreams that would have budded into aspirations, and if given the chance, would have blossomed into her life's ambitions. And, without a doubt, Kerrie would have eventually fallen in love again.

For those of us left behind to always remember and who still mourn, the heart-wrenching, deafening sound of sorrow will forever echo in our hearts the devastating loss of Kerrie's stolen tomorrow.

CHAPTER 2
THE DEAFENING SOUND OF SORROW

My very first "remember where you were" life moment happened on Saturday, October 18th, 1986, at precisely 7:10 p.m. Who knows the exact moment their childhood ends, and what that moment sounds like? I do, and I was fourteen years old.

First, I must go back to the Wednesday before, during a week known to all educators and students as the annual teachers' conference hosted by the Mystery Lake School District in Thompson, Manitoba. For the teachers, the conference provided an opportunity to meet and discuss the curriculum for the upcoming school year, aimed at shaping the future minds of local students. For the students, it was a chance to sleep in, hang out, or party with friends during the three-day holiday weekend, because there were no classes scheduled on Friday.

Instead of partying or hanging out with my friends, I chose instead to board a Grey Goose bus after school on that Wednesday afternoon to take the five-hour bus trip to visit my mother, who I had not seen in months. My parents had separated the year before, and my mother had, in record time, found her third husband and had moved to Flin Flon, Manitoba. Although a tragic (and a very long) story, my parent's divorce did not surprise me, my little brother, or my older sister. Also not shocking was that we had chosen to live with our father in the city where we grew up.

My mother and her third husband (H3) had purchased a two-story house on Green Street, attached to the only laundromat business in Flin Flon. While H3 worked underground at the Hudson Bay Mining and Smelting Company, my mother spent her days running the coin-operated business. The doorbell rang nonstop, with customers requesting loonies or quarters to feed the loud machines that ran continuously from eight a.m. to eleven p.m. A door in the back of the kitchen served as a gateway to the bustling business out front. By day two of my visit, the constant ringing of the doorbell was wearing on my teenage nerves.

On Friday afternoon, as I bent over to gather my wet shoulder-length brown hair into a towel twist, my mother yelled from the bottom of the stairs.

"Katrina phone!"

With one hand gripping another towel in place around my skinny frame, I cracked the bathroom door open to peek down the hallway. I was almost positive H3 was working but I wanted to make sure before tiptoeing down the hallway to their bedroom, where the upstairs phone sat on the nightstand.

"Got it!" I yelled, then picked up the phone and waited for the sharp click that meant the phone downstairs had been hung up.

"Hey, how's it going?" Dan's soft voice tickled my ear from over four hundred kilometres away.

Dan Safflower and I had just started dating. He was a senior in high school and super cute—he was six feet tall and lean, with sea-blue eyes and sandy blond, poker-straight hair that fell past his shoulders with straight-cut bangs. I was surprised to hear from him so soon after we had spent several hours talking on the phone the night before.

"Hey," I greeted him as casually as I could, being half-naked, hiking up the towel above my barely-there boobs. "Good. I was just getting ready to go uptown shopping with my mom." I plopped down on my mother's unmade bed and tugged the towel off my head, releasing my damp hair. "What's up?" I tilted my head to one side and with my other hand, I ran my fingers through my hair, trying to shake it dry.

"Kerrie's missing," he said. "I wanted to tell you before you heard it from someone else."

My hand stopped mid-shake. "What? What do you mean Kerrie's missing? Wasn't she at your place last night?" My mind flashed back to our marathon phone conversation the night before—with the loud music, kids laughing or singing in the background while we talked for hours. A few times Dan had to cover the mouthpiece to yell at someone to, "Stop slamming the door!" which would have annoyed his mother, who had been quietly chaperoning from her bedroom upstairs.

"She was," Dan said, "but then Chad showed up with Lana. I guess Kerrie got upset and left. Nobody's seen her since."

Chad and Lana? When did that happen? Didn't Kerrie and Chad just break up? I frowned at the latest dating update. Kids were always hooking up and breaking up in our close-knit group of friends, which was hard to keep track of. Sometimes there would be break up drama, like a screaming match, an exaggerated display of crying, or—my personal favourite—the punching of a wall. These immature displays of over-exaggerated teenage emotions depended on two things: who was breaking up and how long the relationship had lasted. Both Chad and Kerrie were not the dramatic type; both down-to-earth, level-headed, and shy, plus they had only dated for a week, maybe two, tops. Kerrie was obviously heartbroken if she had wanted to leave the minute Chad showed up with Lana. My heart couldn't help but ache for her—as I knew from personal experience what that felt like. Either way, how the hell could Kerrie be missing? "Did you talk to Rebecca? What is Natalie saying?" I asked.

"Natalie is here. Rebecca is here. They're both *here*. We're *all* here, except for Kerrie," he snapped.

I sat stunned by the sharpness of his tone and bit my lower lip, not knowing what to say.

"We're all splitting up and heading out to go find her. We've made up some posters with her picture on them to hand out around town. The RCMP won't help us. They're telling us that Kerrie has to be missing for at least forty-eight hours before a missing person's report can be..."

"You called the RCMP?" I asked, shocked.

He took a deep breath. "Listen, Katrina, I know how this all sounds, but believe me, *none of us*, not her family, not her friends, knows where Kerrie is. *She is missing.*"

"DAN LET'S GO!" a voice shouted from somewhere in the background.

"I gotta go. I'll call you later," Dan said.

"Wait!"

Dan had already hung up.

Confused, I sat clutching the phone while the dial tone blared in my ear. What the hell was going on? They had contacted the RCMP? They were splitting up to hand out posters around town with Kerrie's picture? I could see them—all my friends piling into either Buddy, Dan, or Bruce's cars to drive around the city streets, only this time, instead of cruising, they were searching for a missing friend. How could not one of them know where Kerrie was? If she had walked home by herself from Dan's house, she could have taken shortcuts through the bush areas. Could she have tripped and possibly hurt herself?

Thompson is littered with small bush areas that have narrow walking trails cutting through them. The short cuts were used often, especially during the cold winter months, to cut down on travel time when on foot. The trails were especially dark at night, and could be treacherous, with low-hanging branches or exposed tree roots. In October, the temperature can go well below freezing. What if she had tripped? I slowly put the receiver back on the cradle as images of Kerrie lying unconscious, injured, and alone in the dark started to play in my head.

"Hurry up Katrina! I'm leaving in fifteen minutes, with or without you!" My mother hollered up the stairs.

"I'll be right down!" I hollered back. I stood up, pushing the thought of Kerrie – possibly injured, unconscious, and alone in the dark—out of my mind. *They'll find her, and when they do, Kerrie will be totally embarrassed by all the drama with the missing person posters and contacting the RCMP. After all, who goes missing in Thompson, Manitoba?* I thought, heading back to my bedroom to get dressed.

***

"Katrina, do you know that girl who's gone missing in Thompson?" my mother asked at the supper table later that night.

With a mouthful of mashed potatoes, I nodded.

H3, with his huge presence, sat eating across from me as my mother fidgeted in her seat between us. He was a large man with broad shoulders, pale skin, sharp features, a pointy nose, and short jet-black hair that looked either wet or oily. I was uncomfortable around him, even though he gave me no reason to. He had hardly been around since I had arrived, working shift work. When he was home, he was either sitting in his lounge chair watching TV or puttering in the laundromat, fixing the machines, barely acknowledging my presence—which didn't bother me one bit. I figured it was because he had no kids of his own or that I looked a lot like my father, with whom he had exchanged an angry word or two (and a fist or two) regarding the mess that was my parent's divorce. As I said, it is a very long, and very dramatic story.

My mother and I were both five feet, five inches tall with a slim build, but that's where our physical similarities ended. My forty-something mother had pale, ghostlike features, sprinkled with fading freckles high on her cheekbones and across her nose, while I had inherited my father's soft brown complexion, thick brown hair, and matching brown eyes. My mother wore her hair short and bleached white-blonde, which made her pale green eyes stand out.

Taking after my dad in the looks department came with a price, as I was "blessed" with his bushy, out-of-control eyebrows that seemed hell-bent on forming one thick unibrow. My only weapon was a pair of tweezers, which I used daily to pluck the stubborn, thick black hairs determined to meet and form a straight line above my nose.

"Katrina!?" My mother's voice was sharp and impatient.

I jerked my head up. "Sorry. What?"

Mom smiled stiffly. "I was just wondering why you've been getting so many calls from *that* boy today. Is it because he's missing you too much?" She winked at me.

I cringed at her lame attempt at teasing me. Usually, I didn't tell my mother a lot about my life, knowing I would eventually regret it, like now. While out shopping that afternoon, and in a moment of weakness, I told her about the tall, cute senior I had just started dating.

I forced a smile and stared down at my plate, not hungry anymore. With the tip of my fork, I pushed the corn away from the roast beef as the mashed potatoes sat heavy in my stomach. "May I please be excused from the table?" I asked politely, putting my fork down.

"But you barely touched your supper," my mother whined.

H3 reached over and patted my mother's arm with his large hand.

"Fine." She sighed dramatically. "I'll wrap it up and put it in the fridge for you for later."

"Thanks, Mom." I gave her my best smile and stood up, leaving my plate where it was.

The room I was staying in had recently been painted a bright white with just enough space for the double bed and small dresser. After closing the door, I fell face down on my unmade bed, shoving my face deep into a pillow to muffle a load groan, desperately wishing I was home with all my friends trying to find Kerrie.

Dan had called later that afternoon just as my mom and I walked through the door from shopping. I dropped my bags and raced to the couch in the living room to snatch up the phone with my shoes still on. My mother said nothing. They had yet to find any sign of Kerrie. They were still out searching for her. He had pulled into the mall parking lot to call me from a payphone in the lobby, so we didn't talk long.

In the confines of my room, I felt trapped as the walls started to close in. I turned onto my back and gazed blankly up at the white ceiling. I felt helpless, then restless, then as if I might burst out of my skin. I got off the bed, cracked open the bedroom door, and stuck my head out. I could hear my mother's muffled voice chatting away nonstop downstairs. I tiptoed down the hallway to her bedroom, took the phone off the nightstand, and sat cross-legged on the floor beside the bed. I put the phone in front of me and dialled Dan's number.

He answered on the first ring.

"Hey." My voice was just above a whisper. "How's it going?"

"Okay, I guess. How are you doing?" The TV was blaring in the background.

"I'm okay. Still no news?" I leaned back against the bed.

"Afraid not. Some of us are here just sitting around trying to watch a movie. A few of us went over to Kerrie's house to sit with her parents. I think her dad is talking to the police tonight."

I wove the curly phone cord between two fingers, pulled the stiff cord straight, then let it go. "Can you talk?" I asked. "I'm kind of going stir crazy here by myself."

"Yeah, hold on." I could hear him move away from the noise of the TV. "Still there?" he asked, shutting his bedroom door. His room was right beside the living room in the basement.

"Yeah, I'm still here."

"I was going to call you." His sweet-sounding soft voice was back.

My heart skipped a beat.

"I'm sorry I snapped at you before," he said.

"It's okay."

"No. It's not okay. It's just that..." His voice cracked.

I bit my lip and waited.

"It's been hell, Kat. How could Kerrie just disappear into thin air? How is that even possible? And what's worse is the RCMP. They won't take us seriously. They shrugged us off, saying she probably ran away or was passed out at a party somewhere. Can you fucking believe that? The longer we wait for them to do something, the longer Kerrie is out there all alone, possibly hurt, or worse." He took a deep, shaky breath.

"I know." I cranked my neck backwards to look up, blinking.

We sat in silence, neither one of us knowing what to say.

"Hey, can you tell me what happened last night?" Trying to break the awkward silence between us. "Maybe it will, I don't know, trigger something important."

"Okay."

For the next hour, I sat in various positions on the floor of my mother's bedroom, listening to Dan as he told his version of what happened last night, before Kerrie disappeared.

The party was no different from any other party he had in his basement. It wasn't really planned; everyone had come together at the last minute. Nobody new showed up, invited or uninvited. There were no arguments or disagreements—just the usual listening to music, singing, dancing, kids telling stories, goofing around, and, of course, there had been drinking. Kerrie was supposed to sleep at Natalie's that night, since her house was just a block and a half away from Dan's house.

The minute Chad and Lana showed up, Kerrie went to find Natalie to tell her she wanted to leave. Natalie agreed, plus it was close to midnight, which was Natalie's curfew. When they reached the top of the stairs, Natalie realized she had forgotten her purse, so she went back down to the basement to get it. Only she was held up by Ron McKenzie, her ex-boyfriend, who wanted to know why she broke up with him the week before.

Ron was a rough-looking guy for his seventeen years, with a weathered complexion, pale blue eyes, and unruly thick short blond hair held down by a ball cap. Natalie and Ron had dated for a little over a month before she dumped him. Truthfully, Ron, a soft-spoken and timid guy, was no match for the free-spirited, "tell it like it is" Natalie—who only wanted to hang out with her friends, party, and have the freedom to have fun. Ron, with the help of a couple of beers, had mustered up enough courage to reach out and gently take Natalie's arm when she passed by him, hoping he could talk her into getting back together. Natalie had no interest in rekindling the relationship and had no problem shouting this into his ear over the loud music.

By the time Natalie broke free from Ron's loose grip, found her purse, and climbed back up the stairs, Kerrie was gone. At first, she thought, Kerrie just went ahead without her, tired of waiting on the small landing with all the shoes at the top of the stairs. So, Natalie left, slamming the back door shut behind her, to follow her best friend's footprints in the fresh snow down the driveway, but Kerrie's trail went cold at the street. Natalie called out Kerrie's name the whole way home.

But there was no sign of Kerrie on the well-lit streets between Spoonbill Crescent and Trout Ave. Drunk and upset, Natalie retraced her steps, thinking they had somehow missed each other. Over the next hour, Natalie wandered the streets searching for her.

"Natalie was pretty drunk, Kat." Dan sighed.

"So what?" It was my turn to snap at him. Did it matter that Natalie was drunk? I didn't think so.

"I'm just saying," he said, defensively. "By the time Natalie got home, it was an hour past her curfew. Her mom could tell right away she had been drinking and was furious with her. When she tried to tell her mom Kerrie was missing and that was the reason for her being so late, her mom thought it was the booze talking and sent her to bed. Mona thought Kerrie had just gone home."

"Was Kerrie drunk?" I asked. Did it matter? Maybe.

"No. None of us think so. She did have a beer, maybe two. When I saw her just before she left, she didn't seem drunk to me, but I wasn't really paying attention. I didn't see her leave because I was on the phone with you." He cleared his throat. "Natalie was the one I was yelling at to either come in or stay out because she kept slamming the backdoor, remember?"

"Yeah, I remember."

"Any way you look at it, it was a fucked-up situation. Kerrie's parents thought she was at Natalie's house. Natalie's mom thought Kerrie had just gone home. Natalie passed out after getting sick and Mona let her sleep in the next morning. It was almost noon before anyone realized Kerrie wasn't at home or at Natalie's house."

He was right, it was a fucked-up situation.

"How's Rebecca doing?" Kerrie's other childhood best friend was a quiet, shy, pretty girl with shoulder-length, thick, dark brown hair. When I first met Rebecca, I was instantly jealous of her God-given perfectly shaped eyebrows above her pale blue eyes.

"She's not good. None of us are. We're all just sitting around, not knowing what else to do. We've called everyone we can think of, stopped anyone we saw on the street today, and walked every route Kerrie could have taken home. The RCMP won't help us until Kerrie's been missing for at least forty-eight hours, which, if you ask me, is a fucking stupid rule. Nobody knows where Kerrie is—not her close friends, not her family. She's missing, for Christ's sake," he said angrily.

I bowed my head as I listened to Dan rant on about how they had searched for Kerrie. Some by car, others on foot, while handing out missing posters with no help from the RCMP.

Kerrie's dad, Jim Brown, went as far as contacting the two local taxicab companies on his own, who willingly told him about any fares that were picked up or dropped off in the Westwood area around Trout Ave that night. This led Mr. Brown on a wild goose chase, knocking on strangers' doors, desperately searching for his fifteen-year-old daughter. I closed my eyes and could picture Kerrie's dad, a short man with thinning, light brown hair, and a potbelly. I knew my father would have done the exact same thing if it had been Jade or me that had gone missing. Only, I was pretty sure my dad wouldn't have knocked.

"Nat's a complete mess," Dan said, changing the subject.

"I would be too." I stretched out my legs and leaned back against the bed. I wasn't surprised Nat was a mess, but it was hard for me to picture her "a mess". The Natalie I knew was a strong-willed girl with fiery brown eyes and long, wild brown hair streaked generously with blonde highlights. She always had an overpowering air of self-confidence about her; within minutes of meeting her, I just knew she would never put up with anyone's bullshit and she had no problem calling a spade a spade. I couldn't help myself but admire her for it and be cautious around her. It was hard to picture the Natalie Dan was describing now—not talking, physically and emotionally exhausted, and visibly deflated. She was clearly blaming herself.

A sudden wave of helplessness came over me, causing a lump to form in my throat. There was nothing I could say or do. For the umpteenth time that day, my brain screamed the same question: Where the hell was Kerrie?

"I wish you were here," Dan lowered his voice.

I swallowed the lump. "Me too," I whispered back.

"Is that my sister?" Jade's voice chirped in the background.

"Yeah," Dan said.

"Hey, sis, how's it going? How's Mom? What's her new boyfriend like?"

Leave it to Jade to be more concerned about our mother's new boyfriend than a missing friend. My sister's white-blonde hair, which matched our mother's, suited her well.

"She's good," I said, purposely ignoring her question about H3.

The last year had not been easy for us while adjusting to our mother being gone. With Dad having to work a lot, it left the household chores and caring for our little brother, Jake, up to my sister and me. The nonstop fighting between our parents over the last few years had been replaced by my sister and me constantly bickering. It also didn't help that we had picked separate sides in the saga surrounding our parents' divorce—Jade was Team Mom, while I was Team Dad. Jade had wanted to come with me to visit Mom, but she had just started a part-time job as a cook at a local restaurant and was scheduled to work over the three-day weekend.

"How could Kerrie have just disappeared?" I asked, purposely changing the subject, but I was curious about what my older sister thought.

"No clue, sis. I got off work at 11:00 p.m. and was at Dan's by 11:30. Kerrie was still here, but I didn't see her leave," Jade said. "Hey, what time will you be home on Sunday?"

"The bus leaves here at nine in the morning. I'm not sure what time it gets in. How's Dad doing?" I held my breath.

"OH! MY! GOD! What do you think? He's batshit crazy, of course!"

I could totally see Jade roll her eyes and frown into the phone. Sounded about right, I thought, but I took her answer with a grain of salt. Jade was known to exaggerate absolutely everything, especially when it came to our dad. They were like oil and water—always battling over curfews, her skipping classes, and how it was his fault that Mom had left us. It was an ongoing war between them, with very little peace time in between their battles. Jade was the spitting image of our mother, only three inches taller and was eighteen months older than me. She was the most overly dramatic person I'd ever known.

"Fair warning Kat, if you thought he was fricken strict before, he's being even more *ridiculous* now. After my shift from work today, I literally had to fight my way out of the house to go out tonight. He wants us both on total lockdown when you get home."

"That's sucks," I said but was still not surprised. At the best of times, Dad was overprotective of his teenage daughters. Now, with a girl our age missing, it would only give him more reason to enforce "his" rules to protect his own girls.

"Okay, I'll give you back to Dan. Say hi to Mom for me."

"I will," I lied, knowing I'd forget the minute I heard Dan's voice again.

"Do you want me to pick you up at the bus depot on Sunday?" Dan asked.

"Sure, that'd be great." My plan was to call a cab since Dad was working the dayshift.

"I'll phone to see what time your bus gets in. Could you let your dad know?"

"Okay," I lied, again. It was just poor timing, and really, there was no good reason to tell my new boyfriend about the dating rules in our house, because there weren't any. Jade and I were forbidden to date until we were sixteen years old and even then, it was "up for discussion". With Kerrie missing and with me dating a senior who also had unlimited access to his family's car, with a spacious backseat, I knew it wouldn't sit well with my dad, especially now. So, for my dad's sake and given everything that was going on, I easily convinced myself to stick with this teenage logic—what Dad doesn't know couldn't hurt him.

***

"Are you planning on sleeping all day?"

My mother's voice jerked me awake from a deep sleep. I sat up and rubbed my eyes, confused about where I was. When it came back to me, I asked, "What time is it?"

She was standing in my bedroom doorway. "It's almost one o'clock. I came to check on you earlier to make sure you were still breathing," she said.

The words "still breathing" felt as if my mother had slapped me wide awake. "Did anyone call?"

"No, sweetheart, there's been no news about your friend. I called a couple of my friends in Thompson this morning, and as far as they know, they still haven't found her. Why don't you get up, and I'll make you breakfast," she said just as the doorbell rang downstairs.

"I'll be right down," I said, but mom was already gone.

Standing at the bathroom sink, I blinked blindly at my reflection before bending over to splash cold water on my face, digging the sleep crust out from the corners of both my eyes. The twelve hours of sleep still felt like a heavy blanket across my shoulders. One more night and I would be home, I told myself, standing up and reaching for my toothbrush in my travel bag.

When the phone came to life on my mother's nightstand, I froze and tilted my head to listen with the toothbrush sticking out of my mouth.

"KATRINA! PHONE!"

I spit out the gob of toothpaste along with my toothbrush into the sink.

"Hello!" I almost shouted into the phone, not bothering to wait for the click and no longer caring about keeping my voice in "cool and casual" new girlfriend mode.

"Hey..." Dan said.

"Did you find her?" I interrupted him, my heart thumping in my ears, even though it was a short sprint from the bathroom.

"No, but..." He cut himself off.

"But? But what?"

"They found a body."

Who knew that one word had the power to make my knees buckle? I sat down hard on my mother's unmade bed.

A body?

I sucked in cool, minty fresh air through my gritted teeth. What exactly did that mean? When a body was found, it meant dead, right? Could a body be found alive? My mind tossed the word around, trying to figure out its meaning.

"Who are *they*?" I asked, surprised at how calm my voice sounded.

"Two women. They were out at the stables this morning riding their horses along the hydro line when they saw someone lying in the bush and called the RCMP." He cleared his throat before continuing. "The only thing we know so far is the body is female."

I closed my eyes to picture it. The hydro line is a wide pathway cleared of trees by the Manitoba Hydro power company so that the power lines could run through the thick northern forest. I knew of the stables and had a rough idea where they were—an out-of-place farm past the Burntwood bridge, not far down the Mystery Lake Highway and down a dirt road. It was a hobby farm where residents could board their horses north of the city.

"You don't think that it could be …" I stopped myself before I said her name. *Don't say her name*, I scolded myself and bit down on my bottom lip, while mentally listing all the reasons why "the body" that "they" had found could not possibly be Kerrie. The stables were at least five kilometres from Dan's house. It just didn't make any sense whatsoever how she could have gotten all the way out there. I wracked my brain trying to remember one conversation where Kerrie, Natalie, or Rebecca ever mentioned horses or horseback riding. Did Kerrie even like horses? I shook my head, convinced there was absolutely no way it could be her.

"Honestly, Kat, I don't know, but I'll call you the minute I hear anything."

There was something wrong. His voice sounded "off" somehow, but I couldn't put my finger on it.

"Wait!" I blurted out, suddenly feeling panicked by the idea of being left alone with my vivid imagination. "When? When do you think you will hear?"

"Not sure," he said, then the line went dead.

I took the phone away from my ear to hold it in front of my face to scowl at it before slamming it back up against my ear. "Dan? Are you still there?"

"Yeah, I'm still here." He cleared his throat.

"What? What are you not telling me?"

"There are a lot of awful rumours flying around town," he whispered.

I pushed the phone harder against my ear to understand him better. "What rumours?" I asked, confused. Why would anyone be spreading rumours?

"That she was beaten to death and..." His voice trailed off.

I shook my head. "Where did you hear that?"

"Never mind." Dan's voice changed its tune. "I shouldn't have said anything. You know how it is in a small town. Rumours are always flying around. I'll call you the minute I hear anything."

"Promise me the minute you hear *anything, anything at all,* you will call me," I pleaded.

"I promise."

I sat for a while, letting what Dan had told me sink in. When I moved to stand up, it hit me, forcing me to sit back down. I realized what had been "off" about Dan's voice. He sounded like he had given up hope.

***

In between dry mouthfuls of cardboard-flavoured Honey Nut Cheerios, I told Mom what Dan said. "He's going to call the minute he hears anything," I said, force feeding myself another spoonful of the tasteless cereal.

She smiled then leaned across the table to pat my arm before getting up to finish the dishes.

For the rest of the day, I kept myself busy by working in the laundry mat, which was pretty easy, seeing it was Saturday, prime time for doing laundry in a small town. Before I knew how, I was exchanging bills for coins, picking up after customers, and wiping down the two long tables used for folding clothes. The tables divided the business right down the middle, with a row of dryers on one side and a row of washing machines on the other.

I scraped the tops of the washing machines, grossed out at the amount of laundry soap scum that built up around the opening where you added the detergent. Another fun fact I learned about the public while cleaning the small washroom: people had no aim when it came to putting wet paper towels in the wastebasket or pee in the toilet, which tested my gag reflexes.

Later in the afternoon, Mom went to the convenience store two doors down to rent us a couple of VHS movies to watch. My mother chose the recently released *The Goonies,* about a bunch of kids in search of hidden treasure, trying to lighten my mood and keep me from staring at the phone beside the couch, willing it to ring.

When the phone did ring, my mother paused the movie as I held my breath from my spot in H3's large leather recliner. Breathing again when she shook her head at me as she politely told the caller that she couldn't talk right now, because she was expecting an important call and needed to keep the line free.

Hope continued to beat steadily in my chest with each passing hour as the afternoon dragged on. What was that saying? No news was good news? If at any point my mind tried to argue with my heart with the idea that *the body* was Kerrie's, under my breath, I would repeat the reasons why it couldn't be her, whether I was scraping the globs of scum off those washing machines, mopping up the pee around the toilet, or watching those kids try to find that hidden treasure.

After supper, I was clearing the dishes when the phone rang in the living room, which for some odd reason startled me, seeing as I was waiting for it to ring most of the day. I stood frozen in place and glanced up at the clock that hung above the kitchen table. It was 7:10 p.m. My mother pulled the plates from my grasp, and with a slight nod, motioned for me to go and answer it. H3 wasn't home from work yet.

When the receiver touched my ear, I opened my mouth to say "Hello" but frowned instead, confused by what I was listening to. No voice greeted me from the other end. All I heard was wailing, screaming, and sobbing. It was a god-awful sound, a grief ridden sound. It was the sound of all my friends crying back home. When I deciphered the meaning of what I was listening to, I felt as if I had been punched in the stomach.

My knees buckled. I sat down hard on the couch, then leaned forward and covered my mouth with one hand while the knuckles of my other hand turned white as I gripped the phone receiver. I sat completely stunned as I listened to the horrific sound of some screaming, some sobbing, and some crying coming from all my friends back home–it was heartbreaking.

"OH God Kat, it was her! Kerrie is dead!" Dan's voice exploded in my ear.

Dan's words confirmed what I already knew, but his voice made me sit up, letting my hand fall limp in my lap. I opened my mouth to speak, then closed it. What should I say? What could I say? I searched my brain, desperate to find the right words, but there was only one word that came to mind, only it got stuck in my throat.

NO.

No, this can't be happening. No, it can't be Kerrie. No, there had to be some mistake.

No. NO! NO!

So, I said nothing. Instead, I shook my head and hung up the phone. Selfishly cutting myself off from the deafening sound of sorrow being sung by all my friends back home.

I sat trying to convince myself it was Kerrie, forcing myself to believe it was really her. That the cold, lifeless body found out in the woods was actually her, while my teenage brain struggled to understand what exactly that meant.

I leaned forward and covered my face with my hands as an eerie calmness spread through me. I felt oddly numb and hollow at the same time, like some part of me was gone. Only, I wasn't sure what part. What felt even more weird was that I had no urge to cry. My eyes blinked dry, with no tears threatening to come. *Was this what grief felt like?*

When my mother's arms wrapped around me, I instinctively fell into them, letting her pull me close and hug me hard. The smell of her perfume brought back brief flashes of my childhood, when she had the power to make the pain go away and make everything okay with a hug or a kiss. I clung to her, feeling the innocence of my childhood slipping away, now understanding that my own mother was powerless to make this pain stop, and that nothing was going to be okay ever again.

And still, I did not cry.

CHAPTER 3
SUMMER OF 1986

The day after Kerrie's body was found, I was back on that Grey Goose bus to go home. I chose a seat five rows from the back, in the smoking section, that was far enough away from the bathroom to avoid the potent fumes that would eventually perfume the air during the five-hour trip. I dropped my overstuffed backpack with my new clothes on the aisle seat and fell into the seat next to the window. After wiggling out of my parka, I leaned my head against the cool glass of the window, closed my eyes and inhaled diesel fumes, trying to mentally prepare myself for the long ride home. When the bus lurched forward, followed by a loud hissing sound, I opened my eyes and was relieved to see the seat beside me had remained empty, as intended with my strategically placed backpack.

When the bus turned onto the highway, I slipped off my boots, pulled my knees up to my chest and wrapped my arms around them, hugging them tightly. I stared out the window, listening to the other passengers settle in around me. I still had not cried. Not one tear. Even with the heart-wrenching song of sorrow playing on a continuous loop inside my head. I felt oddly calm, Kerrie's body, discovered in the woods, still did not seem real to me.

As I watched the passing scenery, I saw the familiar rock formations that would suddenly appear and then disappear as the bus sped past. Rocks cliffs without warning sprouted out of the forest floor, making brief appearances within the treeline on either side of the roughly patched highway. Some had been spray painted with large sloppy letters in various sizes and colours on the uneven surfaces to memorialize a relationship in an uneven heart or the year of a graduating class. The graffiti was out of place against the backdrop of the dark green spruce and pine trees with poplar trees popping up here and there, standing tall and proud, wearing their bright white bark and displaying their yellow and orange leaves, showing off their autumn colours. The moving northern landscape captured within the window frame of the bus seemed different to me somehow.

I knew the bush like the back of my hand, having grown up surrounded by the mystery of it my entire life. As a young kid, it had been my very own private playground where I would spend hours exploring its nooks and crannies in search of fairies, goblins, or trolls, only to startle the odd rabbit or two.

The treeline that surrounded Thompson was only a couple blocks from my home, where I would drop my bike carelessly at the treeline and hit the ground, running to enter this mystical world, which would always swallow me whole.

I closed my eyes and leaned my head back against the headrest, trying to let the movement of the bus lull me to sleep.

To me, the forest had always been a wondrous place, a safe place. I remember feeling so small underneath the protection of the tallest spruce trees, surrounded by the thick, wild bush and breathing in deep the beauty of it all. My sneakers would sink into the mossy forest floor, soaking my running shoes right through to my socks. While exploring, I would have to duck under low-hanging branches and jump over strategically placed tree roots running down narrow pathways, which would always lead me to some babbling brook or a lazy stream.

These childhood memories now brought with them a feeling of disappointment, like I had figured out how a magic trick worked. My innocent perception of the woods was disappearing as the vivid memories of the vibrant colours turned to a dull grey, casting dark shadows on the forest floor, creating shades of suspicion. I could now see the ominous possibilities that the northern woods had to offer, with its ability to camouflage horrific secrets of heinous crimes within its dense foliage—like the murder of a teenage girl.

I opened my eyes, blinking back into focus the trees along the highway which had turned into a mishmash of green, orange, and yellow colours, all under the cover of an overcast grey sky.

My stomach growled in protest at my earlier decision to skip the breakfast my mother had offered. I had hoped to curl up and sleep the whole way home, but that hope was fading fast as I sat restless. When Kerrie's smiling, pretty-cute face flashed before my eyes. I took a sharp breath in as my head whispered to my heart: Kerrie is dead. This thought was followed by missing, beaten and murdered—which made me dizzy. These words didn't belong in my limited teenage vocabulary. How did Kerrie get from Dan's house to the stables? Did she know who did this to her? Did she go willingly, or was she taken?

I wracked my brain, trying to remember the last time I had seen her. When the memory came back to me, I sat up straight, as if preparing to catch it. I turned my head to the window to watch the memory replaying like a movie scene in the glass's reflection. I saw myself walking down the crowded hallway of the high school, on my way to meet Dan in the forum for lunch.

The forum was the meeting place for all students in the high school and was on the first floor. It was a large open area the size of four classrooms put together with a large circle carved into the cement floor in the middle, with two wide steps leading to the circle's centre. The entire area was covered in the ugliest shade of stretched-thin orange carpet. It was the main hang-out spot for students during lunch period, a spare or a skipped class, especially during the winter months, when it wasn't worth the effort or time it took to warm up a vehicle to leave the school grounds. At any given time during the hours of 8: 30 a.m. to 3:40 p.m., students from all grades could be found sprawled out to eat, do last-minute homework assignments, study, or play a card game or two. A small convenience store that doubled as a teaching tool for business classes, conveniently sat right beside it, with various items for sale, like school hoodies, T-shirts, school supplies, drinks, and microwavable snacks like pizza pops for a quick lunch.

As I wove my way through the crowd of kids, I caught a glimpse of the top of Kerrie's blond curly head bobbing up and down. She was kneeling in front of her half-locker in the section assigned to all grade ten students, digging for something. When I was right behind her, I stopped to nudge her gently with my knee with just enough force to make her lose her balance and fall headfirst into that half-locker. When she scrambled out, her head snapped upwards, obviously annoyed, but her expression changed when she saw my smiling face and the corner of her mouth turned up slightly. "Hey, Kat! You bugger!" She had laughed, shaking a fist up at me.

An icy chill ran down my spine as I crossed my arms and squeezed hard, trying to silence the chord the memory had struck. Kerrie was small enough to fit into that stupid half-locker. She could have easily been *taken*.

I squinted suspiciously at the passing forest, thinking Kerrie would have been so cold all alone in the woods at night. An image suddenly popped into my head of her smoky breath disappearing into the chilly night air while she lay on the partially frozen ground into my head. Was she still alive when they left her? Did she know she was going to die?

My hands shot up to cover my face just as a passenger walked by, heading for the bathroom. I squeezed my eyes shut, feeling a sharp pain in my heart that was spreading across my entire chest, making it hard to breathe. Visions of Kerrie, all by herself, alone out in the woods, invaded my thoughts. I shook my head, like an Etch-A-Sketch, trying desperately to erase the images. Then I rubbed my face hard with both hands—*think about something else, anything else,* I begged myself.

***

Certain things about my hometown I don't remember being told. I just knew. I cannot explain how I knew; I just did. For instance, I knew the very existence of the city relied solely on the vast amount of nickel deposits The International Nickel Company of Canada mined, smelted, refined, then shipped out across both provincial and international borders. Everyone in town called the mine INCO, except my little brother, who on many occasions would announce loudly that our dad worked at INCO STINKO!

The nonstop mining operation made the air in the city smell and taste like sulphur. The taste was gross, like lighting a match, blowing out the flame, then putting the smoking stick on your tongue.

I do remember rolling my eyes while doodling on the front of my binder in my grade nine geology class when the nerdy teacher, a retired geologist with thick, silver hair and black-rimmed glasses, taught the significance of the mine to our town. He outlined INCO's importance to the very survival of Thompson, teaching us with academic enthusiasm what the prosperous mine had done for both the conception and continued growth of our northern Manitoba town. Not to mention how it would provide employment for many future generations to come with the large amounts of the purest nickel deposits in the world just beneath our feet. I jumped in my seat, startled, when he clapped his hands together to emphasize this exciting tidbit of information, which also woke up a couple of other students from their educational induced comas.

The worst things about living in Thompson were the long cold winters and the isolation one felt by being in the palm of the north's winter grip. The start of the coldest season would begin a few short weeks after school started in the fall and would carry on well into April, sometimes reaching into May.

Before I was old enough to form a proper sentence, I knew what "wind chill" meant, and what it was capable of. The deadly northern wind could not only plummet temperatures far below the freezing mark, but it also had the infinite power to bite off exposed human skin in a matter of seconds.

What was even more absurd was that the one and only high school and six elementary schools would stay open for classes, no matter how low below the freezing mark the temperature dropped. Students and teachers alike were always expected to show up for classes even when their vehicles had dug their tires in and refused to start after being plugged in for hours.

After accumulating copious amounts of snow, which was easily sustained by the consistent below-freezing temperatures, the feeling of isolation would soon creep in, because it was just too damn cold to do anything outdoors. There would be no ice skating, tobogganing, ice fishing, skiing, or snowmobiling like the travel pamphlet boasted because of the short time it took for the wind chill to attack and snap off exposed skin. Residents would have no other choice but to hunker down inside their homes, with only two local radio stations and two TV channels connecting them to the outside world.

Next to being surrounded by the beauty and majestic scenic northern forest, the best thing about living in Thompson was, and would always be, the spectacular aurora borealis: the northern lights. Mother Nature's light show was proof of her very existence, pitching light against darkness. I have so many childhood memories of being ripped, half asleep, from the warmth of my bed in the middle of the night—most times in the dead of winter—to wake wrapped in my father's arms while he stood on our front porch, pointing to a sky lit up by Mother Nature's show. Even with the wind chill reaching under my thin nightgown and nipping at my bare legs, I would gasp and squeal in awe, mesmerized by all the different colours of nature's palette flashing high above us—blues, greens, yellows, and reds—as they danced wildly against the black backdrop of the northern sky.

During the cool summer months, I would jump on my bike and ride on city streets with their unique circular design that always steered me back onto Thompson Drive, which was the main circle street within city limits that gave access to all six residential areas. Each of these areas in Thompson had their own distinct name: Riverside, Westwood, Deerwood, Juniper, Burntwood, and Eastwood. These six sections were large enough to each have their own elementary school, which taught students from kindergarten to grade eight. I also just knew that Riverside was the rich area of town, where Eastwood was the poor area, with the other areas falling somewhere in between, representing the middle class.

On the northwest side, the Riverside area ran alongside the always-moving and impressive Burntwood River. On my bike, I would zip down streets named after minerals mined locally, like Nickle Road, Copper Road, Silver Crescent, and Cobalt Crescent, always impressed by the mansion-sized homes with their large and well-manicured lawns.

My short legs never made it as far as the Eastwood area because it was on the other side of town from where I lived. I knew, having driven through the area enough times, that Eastwood had the tallest apartment buildings, with townhouses, and rental properties on streets named after prominent academic universities like Yale Ave, Oxford Bay, Cambridge Street, and Harvard Street.

On the southwest side was the Westwood area, with streets cleverly named after fish commonly caught in the northern lakes that surrounded Thompson such as Trout Ave, Sturgeon Crescent, Pike Crescent, and Rainbow Crescent.

The Burntwood area, which was right beside the Westwood area and on the city's south end, had some streets named in Cree, that were not easy to pronounce unless practised, like Mitishto Bay, Wuskwatim Bay, and Notigi Bay.

On the far east side of the town was the Juniper area, with its roads named after locally grown trees, like Birch Avenue, Walnut Avenue, and Elm Street.

The Deerwood area, right next to the Juniper area, on the southeast side, had streets named after wildlife, such as Caribou Road, Lynx Crescent, and Elk Bay.

For the first nine years of their academic life, students attended the elementary school depending on which area of town they lived in. There were two grade eight classes in each elementary school, with roughly twelve students per class, averaging twenty-five elementary school graduates each spring. So, with six elementary schools averaging twenty-five grade eight graduates, this would roughly come to one hundred and fifty *new* high school students walking through the front lobby of the local high school each fall.

RD Parker Collegiate High School was a large and intimidating building located right on Thompson Drive. Within its two-story walls, it could accommodate over a thousand students each school year. Some of these students came from the many surrounding reserves, like Wabowden, Shamattawa, or Nelson House, increasing the student population and adding to the diversity of the student body taught within its many classrooms.

It was a mystery to me how twenty kids from grade nine to grade twelve, who came from different areas of Thompson, found each other and became good friends, but that was what happened in the summer of 1986. We were a tight-knit group of kids who were just trying to navigate the challenges of our teenage existence, leaning on each other through heartbreaks, family dramas, friendship dilemmas, and our overall exaggerated, over-inflated teenage problems. Of course, there were smaller, closer friendships that existed within the larger group that had unbreakable bonds, like Kerrie, Natalie, and Rebecca. But whenever there was a house party to go to or a car to climb in to cruise the city streets, we all seemed to gravitate towards each other for some mysterious reason.

The story of how I became part of this unlikely group of friends could be traced back to 1969, when my twenty-year-old father left his hometown of Winnipeg, Manitoba, to venture north in search of a steady job. On his own, my dad took Highway 6 north, past the fifty-fifth parallel, to start his new life in a city nicknamed the Hub of the North, which was etched below Thompson's name on the sign just as you entered city limits.

In 1975, with his bare hands, my father built an-A frame log cabin-style home on Notigi Bay in the Burntwood area. It was a three-bedroom bungalow with a large bay window in the front and, in its centre, an enormous stone fireplace. My childhood home was nicknamed the "Gingerbread House" by all my friends because of its uncanny resemblance to the edible gingerbread structure, especially in December, when it was lit up with over a hundred multicoloured lights during the Christmas season.

Dad worked his way up in the mine from a labourer position to a furnace operator in the smelter department while Mom slung beer at a local bar called the Steel Centre. After fourteen years, their marriage abruptly ended, leaving my father to raise his two teenage daughters and his eleven-year-old son all on his own.

At six foot two with broad shoulders, sharp weathered features, and thinning brown hair brushed forward to cover his receding widow's peak, my dear old dad was just getting his bearings as a single father the previous summer. If anyone asked him why he had fought like hell to keep his three kids, he would answer without hesitation that he wouldn't have had it any other way.

Single parenting proved challenging for our dad, with him having to work full time while trying to keep track of his children, especially his daughters. His work schedule consisted of a twenty-eight-day shift rotation, with eight-hour shifts on days, afternoons, and nights, and varying days off in between. This forced him to be clever in enforcing his many house rules. He learned how to use the telephone to monitor and manage curfews, calling us at the exact moment we were supposed to be walking through the front door—not just then, but many, many times during his shifts. There was no pattern to his phone call check-ins. It could be five times in an hour, two times in half an hour, or once on the hour. He would even call five minutes after we had just talked to him. It was his way of making sure his girls were home safe and sound, but more importantly, that we stayed home.

Jade and I tried our best to predict when he would call, but we could never figure out the craziness of his sporadic phone check-ins. Just when we thought it was safe to put our shoes back on and go out again, he would call again! What we knew for sure was that if we were NOT physically home to answer his phone call, "there would be hell to pay." The first part of that hell would be him leaving work in the middle of his shift to come home, followed by hours of loud lecturing in the kitchen that always ending with a lengthy grounding sentence.

Add to this the inconvenience of having to take care of our eleven-year-old brother, Jake. One of us always had to be home to watch him, so it only made perfect teenage sense we should start throwing house parties of our own.

Of course, the parties started out small at first, with us just having a "few" kids over, but like in most small towns, word travelled fast. A few kids quickly grew into a house full of kids in an impressively short period of time. Our clever father would never know how many of our friends knew his work schedule off by heart or how many of them had guzzled a beer sitting in his favourite spot on the couch. That was how Jade and I met and became a part of this tight-knit group of kids, because each one of them, at some point during the summer of 1986, walked through the front door of the Gingerbread House on Notigi Bay.

Another parenting tactic Dad used to try to catch us doing something wrong was what Jade and I referred to as the "Fake-Out". A hint that this might be happening was when he was working the night shift and would leave the house around 9:30 p.m. to first go for coffee at a popular coffee shop. My sister and I would become suspicious if he started to complain a little too much and a little too loudly about having to go to work while packing his steel lunchbox before slamming it shut to head out the door reluctantly.

The first time the Fake-Out happened, my sister and I were impatiently watching the clock, knowing a couple cars filled with our friends were parked a block away in the empty parking lot at Burntwood School. Later, we would come to find out our dad had already asked for the night off. Instead of going to work, he went to his favourite coffee shop in the Southwood Mall to sip cups of coffee, biding his time before returning home to catch us hosting one of our teenage gatherings. We narrowly escaped that first time, thanks to a mechanical problem with his 1979 gold Lincoln Town Car, which we could hear coming from blocks away because of its loose and loud muffler that he couldn't afford to fix, giving us just enough time to clear the house. Kids bolted out the back door just as our dad sashayed through the front door, with a look of "AH HA" written all over his face, which quickly turned to disappointment.

The Gingerbread House was just over fourteen hundred square feet, with a large living room that stretched almost across the front of the house, covered by a vaulted ceiling with a bay window that overlooked Notigi Bay. The house's best feature was the black-and-white stone fireplace, surrounded by well-worn brown furniture that matched the thick brown carpet.

A floor-model record player sat in the corner of the large living room. During our parties, we would blast hit songs of the day from popular bands like Mötley Crüe, Bon Jovi, Heart, or Chicago on vinyl records that Jade and I bought with our weekly allowances. The band Alabama was one of our favourites. As soon as that harmonica began to play at the beginning of "Mountain Music", we would all jump up when that old man started to speak: "You see that mountain over there? Yeah, I am going to climb that mountain." Songs like "Fishing in the Dark" and "Hotel California" had the same effect, making us stop whatever we were doing to dance and sing along, all of us out of tune.

When the phone rang, everyone knew the drill. I would climb over kids to get to the phone, cringing when someone dragged the needle across one of our records to stop it from playing, even though turning down the volume would have worked just as well. Within seconds, the party atmosphere was replaced by kids shushing each other.

"BE QUIET, EVERYONE!" I would yell a final warning with my hand on the phone receiver, only picking it up when I was sure everyone in all the rooms of the house knew to be quiet.

"Hi, Dad," I answered, my voice fine-tuned with the just right amount of teenage annoyance. "Yeah, yeah, we're all home," I sighed. "Yes, Jake is in bed." This wasn't a total lie. Jake was in bed—just not in his own bed. My baby brother, with his crewcut blond hair and green eyes, was in heaven, safely tucked out of our way in our dad's bed, surrounded by junk food, his favourite books, and late-night TV shows.

Sometimes Dad would work a "double shift" which he rarely turned down when asked, because of the much-needed overtime pay. Another challenge with being a single parent was it was a never-ending struggle for him to support us with only one income. When this happened, I would give the thumbs-up sign, and after hanging up, a loud cheer would erupt throughout the house because the party could then carry on well past midnight.

There were never any drugs at our parties, an unspoken rule that was not broken, no matter where the party was held. Alcohol was a different story. We would pool our money together to buy a couple of two-fours of Labatt's Lite, Club, or OV beer, and sometimes a litre of Baby Duck wine, using the oldest-looking guy in the group to get it.

The beer runs usually fell on the broad shoulders of Eugene Oliver, who everyone called Geno. My dad once described him as being "built like a brick shithouse" because Geno stood an inch shorter than Dad, and who could easily pass for eighteen. At seventeen years old, he kept his impressively thick black beard trimmed close to his chubby cheeks, with sideburns that connected his generous facial hair to his short, wavy black hair and matching brown eyes. The best and worst thing about Geno was his size. To his very core, Geno was a bully, using his wide girth and deep voice to push around kids to get what he wanted or to intimidate anyone stupid enough to challenge him. He could be very intimidating, and I had witnessed him being unkind, even cruel to kids, both in and out of our group. There were many times—under my breath, of course—I had called him an asshole.

On the rare occasion Geno did get asked to show some ID, Geno being Geno, would confidently claim he had left his wallet at home, then head out to the parking lot in search of the most vulnerable residents in our city. Homeless people were always loitering outside popular bars, like the Burntwood Hotel or the Trappers Tavern, stopping patrons coming in and out to ask for either money or a beer to quench their thirst. With Geno's power of persuasion, he could always convince one of these poor souls to "pull" beer for him, returning the favour with either a buck or a beer.

Geno was also the guy you wanted on your side if ever a fight broke out. He did double duty as a bouncer at our parties if an uninvited guest showed up, which didn't happen very often. But when it did, all Geno had to do was puff out his massive chest and, in his loud, bravado voice, either send the uninvited guest away or break up the fight—something he always managed to do. I truly believed if the mafia ever set up shop in Thompson, Manitoba, Geno would be recruited as one of their top lieutenants.

Most of our parties that summer were held either at the Gingerbread House or in Dan's basement on Trout Ave. Dan was blessed with two parents who seemed okay with having their basement filled with loud, singing teenagers drinking alcohol every other weekend. The only catch was the parties had to be chaperoned, usually by Dan's mother, who was upstairs quietly reading or watching TV.

The smaller, close-knit friendships within the group were determined by where each one of us lived in proximity to one another or, more importantly, by who owned or had regular access to a car.

Dave Hancock, or "Buddy" as everyone called him, lived in the Deerwood area and was often given permission to drive his family's light brown Plymouth Satellite, a giant beast of a car. This allowed him to taxi around kids like Natalie, Rebecca, and Kerrie, who lived in the Eastwood area. Buddy, a shy guy, was short and stocky, with curly black hair that peaked out from under the ball cap he always wore. If anyone ever asked me what Buddy's real name was, I would have to stop to think for a minute to try to remember it. His nickname covered him like a second skin, because it suited him so well. Buddy was a good friend to everybody and was a kind soul who could never hurt a fly.

Before I fell for Dan, I had first noticed Bruce Landon. At seventeen, he was tall and lean, with an athletic build, and ambitious enough to have saved money, all on his own, to buy a burgundy Dodge Daytona. The compact sporty car wasn't as big as Buddy's boat, which limited how many kids could fit in it, but it served its purpose by transporting kids from point A to point B when needed. Bruce, with his military crewcut, black hair, blue eyes, and pale complexion, was well-respected and well-liked within our group. He acted much older than his teenage years, likely because he was raised by a hardworking single mother in a modest house in the Juniper area.

When the Grey Goose bus shifted roughly into lower gear, it jerked me forward in my seat, then back to the present. Pushing my cheek up against the glass where I could peer in between the windows and the rows of seats in front of me to see what was up ahead. It was Fiddler's Corner, the left turn the bus had to make to get onto Highway 39 to continue north. I repositioned my butt on the seat and pulled my parka around my shoulders. There were four hours left to go on the trip.

The girls in our group were an equal mix of sugar and spice, all with similar interests and common likes and dislikes with music, movies, and clothes. Some girls chose the over-the-top poofy hairstyles, while others wore their hair straight with bangs. Some wore no makeup, while others wore thick blue eyeliner to match the flavour of the day heavy blue eye shadow.

Most of the girls were quiet and shy, but a select few were loud and outspoken, like Natalie and Betty Lamb. Betty was a high-spirited, short, chubby girl with long brown hair always back-combed high around and above her round face, wildly falling loose halfway down her back. She had an impressive Newfy accent that spiced up her English. Her loud cackling laugh could sometimes hurt my ears.

Janis Leblanc fit nicely into the shy and quiet mould. She was pretty but a plain girl with brown wavy shoulder-length hair and a pale complexion splattered with just the right number of freckles. The soft-spoken fifteen-year-old girl, for reasons I would never understand, dated Geno that summer.

My best friend was Tammy Barnes. The thought of Tammy brought with it a slight pang of guilt, making me shift to a more comfortable position in my seat, because I didn't call her once over the weekend. From talking to Dan, I knew Tammy had been at his party the night Kerrie went missing, that she had joined the search party the next day, and that she had been one of those voices wailing in sorrow.

Tammy and I met earlier on last summer at one of Bruce's house parties, and shortly after, we became inseparable. She was a year ahead of me in school and lived in the Deerwood area with her parents and Carly, her younger sister, who also hung out with the group from time to time. Tammy wore her long, silky blonde hair loose, falling halfway down her back with straight-cut bangs. Her larger-than-life smile always showed off her perfectly straight white teeth.

My best friend could be very naïve, so much so that she was teased relentlessly for it within the group, often being called a "typical dumb blond." Once, she accepted Bay Buck coupons instead of cash from a customer to pay for a meal at the restaurant where she worked part time as a waitress. I choked back a chuckle, remembering how she had complained to me about it afterward. Her blue eyes went wide in disbelief, because she just couldn't believe how unfair it was that her boss was deducting the amount she had accepted in the local in-store coupons from her next paycheck. How was she supposed to know? Her innocent way of thinking and her inability to speak badly about anyone was what I loved most about her. Where Buddy wouldn't hurt a fly, Tammy would catch that fly and go out of her way to drive miles just to release it. I promised myself I would call her the minute I got home, to check in and see how she was holding up with everything that was going on.

I wiggled my butt on the hard seat and found myself missing the soft, plush seats in Dan's car. The thought of my boyfriend made me smile.

At the beginning of the summer, I would climb into the back of Dan's brown Pontiac Parisian, with its soft beige material seats. By the end of September, I sat up front in the middle, right next to him, with no space between us. This was because he would purposely take a sharp turn every chance he got while yelling "COD corner!" which stood for "Come Over Dear". This clever driving manoeuvre would always make me fall towards him, sometimes almost onto his lap.

When Tammy told me she heard Dan had a crush on me, that's when I first noticed how cute he was. Not only was he cute, but he was also smart, funny, witty, and a true romantic. After only a week of dating, I would find poems scribbled in his handwriting on scraps of paper stuffed into my jacket pockets. He was also a natural at playing the guitar and would sometimes call me late at night to play songs he had been practicing for hours. When he mastered "Stairway to Heaven", I would fall asleep listening to him play with the phone beside my ear on the pillow. Dan and I officially started dating on October 2nd.

The Thompson Billiards, or the TB as everyone in town called it, was the place to be on any night of the week. If Jade and I weren't sure of what was going on that night, and Dad was settled into his favourite spot on the couch to watch a hockey game, we would walk the eight blocks uptown to the popular pool hall.

The TB was in the basement of the same building as The Stage, one of the two movie theatres downtown. At the bottom of the steep, slippery, ceramic-tiled stairs, the large billiard room was big enough for a dozen pool tables and two snooker tables. A variety of video games and pinball machines also lined one wall. An older man with thinning white hair monitored the timers, collected the money for the pool tables, and ran the concession stand. It was a teenager's paradise, and, of course, my father hated the place, forbidding my sister and me from stepping one foot in it. That didn't stop Jade and me from spending countless hours playing eight-ball pool or beating the top score on the Pac-Man or Frogger arcade games.

When everyone showed up at the TB and realized we had no other place to go, we would split up and jump into either Bruce, Buddy, or Dan's cars to cruise around town. On those summer nights, with the windows rolled down, we drank slushes bought with spare change dug out of the car's ashtray. We would crank up the volume to sing along with the top forty hits, with songs like "You Give Love a Bad Name" by Bon Jovi or "Papa Don't Preach" by Madonna, played by the CHTM radio station.

Sometimes and without warning, a challenge to a drag race would be made when another vehicle filled with teenagers who were also cruising around town would pull up beside us at a red light. When the car revved its engine, then let off the brakes only to slam on them again, which caused the vehicle to lurch forward. If the challenge was accepted, both cars would head south of the city, driving a few kilometres down Highway 6 to a straight stretch of highway known as the Quarter Mile. Someone had even taken the time to spray-paint a "start" and "finish" line on the uneven road surface. Kids would scramble out of cars to line the highway near the finish line, ready to cheer on either Dan, Bruce, or Buddy. With his souped-up golden brown Chevy Nova, Ron McKenzie was the long-standing champion that summer.

When cruising around aimlessly induced a collective boredom among us, we would meet up in one of the two mall parking lots to figure out a game to play.

Car tag was a favourite, and the most fun. It was based on the original game of tag, but instead of kids running around in an open field, inexperienced teenagers drove vehicles, with the playing field being any street within city limits. Once we were equally distributed between cars, one car would become "IT", by a simple coin toss. A football could be used to throw and tag the other vehicle, but with our combined teenage intelligence, we assigned a "Jumper" to each car instead. The reason being was a football could accidentally hit an unsuspecting vehicle that wasn't in play, which could cause an accident. The Jumper's role was to get out of the car, even if the car was moving, to tag the other vehicles.

Sometimes all the cars in play would be stuck at an intersection at a red light. The Jumpers from each car would have to run back and forth and in between vehicles, tagging the other car—waiting for the light to turn green. Meanwhile, the other kids hung out the car windows, screaming and yelling, cheering the Jumpers on. If a car not in play happened to be stuck among us at the red light, that driver would watch wide-eyed, confused, wondering what the hell these stupid teenagers were doing. Car Tag wasn't always that exciting, because there could be countless hours and litres of gas spent driving aimlessly around town without meeting up with another car in play for hours.

Car surfing was the most idiotic game that one guy in the group had dreamed up. It was less popular than car tag, mainly because few kids could or would play it. McCreedy Park was a small campground tucked within the trees north of the city, past the Burntwood bridge and Popeyes, a few kilometres down the Mystery Lake Highway. The unmonitored campground had a narrow, winding road running through it, with access to about twenty campsites.

At the campground's entrance, one guy—never one of the girls—would climb onto the roof of a car, strike a pose like a surfer with arms outstretched, knees bent, and bare feet clinging to the hot roof. When that guy screamed "Ready!" the driver would drive, slow at first, but then increase the speed as much as the narrow road would allow. The surfer would struggle to keep his balance, dodging low-hanging tree branches and sharp corners. Eventually, that guy would either be knocked off or have no other choice but to jump off, narrowly missing a tree branch. He would walk away with a few bumps, bruises, and a scrape or two, dusting himself off while the other kids cheered at his stupidity. Not one of those guys made it to the end of that narrow dirt road that summer, but it wasn't for lack of trying.

Santa Maria Pizza was the favourite late-night hot spot. The popular Italian restaurant was the only place in town open twenty-four hours, making it our go-to place after a night of partying, when one of us craved the best pizza in town.

Our group were also regulars at the popular coffee spot, Chicken Chef, where the owners would let us sit for hours, drinking bottomless cups of coffee while taking up to four tables in the smoking section. During these coffee sessions, we would discuss and sometimes have heated debates about the news or world events. Fries and gravy were a staple for all of us, especially Rebecca and Tammy, who would order a plate of the crispy fries smothered in the dark brown gravy only to then blanket it with a thick layer of black pepper. I would watch, horrified, as they unscrewed the cap off the small glass pepper shaker to free pour.

The thought of food made my stomach growl once again, making me fidget in my seat. Giving up on getting any sleep, I sat up straight and put my sock feet on my boots to avoid the germ-infested bus floor. Ponton, Manitoba, a small gas station an hour outside of Thompson, was just up ahead, and was on the bus schedule as one of the rest stops. I tried to ignore my sudden craving for fries and gravy, to instead convince myself to want the day-old egg salad sandwich—which wasn't too bad for a gas station out in the middle of nowhere.

I silently urged the bus to go faster, impatiently wanting to get home to see *all* my friends.

Then it hit me.

Kerrie would not be with them.

This harsh new reality made my chest spontaneously tighten, forcing an involuntary gasp to escape loudly from my lips. Horrified and embarrassed by the sound I had just made, I turned to face the window, away from any passengers who might have heard me. Kerrie's pretty-cute face stared right back at me in the window's reflection.

I started to shake as clear and vivid memories of Kerrie flooded my mind, as if some emotional dam had just broken apart inside of me. I saw her walking through the front door of the Gingerbread House, laughing with Natalie and Rebecca. I saw her lying flat on her stomach in the forum, knees bent up with her feet dangling above her butt, playing cards with Buddy, Bruce, and Natalie, screaming "Asshole!" at the top of her lungs. I saw her sitting cross-legged on the floor in Dan's basement, swaying back and forth while singing "Hotel California". I saw her sitting on Natalie's lap in the brown recliner, their heads bowed, foreheads touching, giggling at a secret only best friends shared. I saw her blond curly head poking up over the back seat of Buddy's car, wide-eyed and smiling, waiting anxiously for Car Tag to start. I saw her shooting pool at the TB, scratching on the eight ball, squealing loudly in defeat. I saw her kneeling in front of her locker, smiling up at me, shaking her fist. And then finally, the most painful image of all—Kerrie's lifeless body lying under the dark October night sky, left out in those dark woods to die—alone.

The memories of Kerrie faded out of focus and became blurred as the tears finally came. I slapped a hand over my mouth to stifle any more sounds of my solo song of sorrow as a sudden wave of grief crashed over me. Feeling helpless and unable to control my emotions, I leaned forward and covered my face with both hands, digging my elbows into my knees, trying to muffle my sobs.

When I finally managed to calm myself down and pull some resemblance of myself back together, I sat up and took a deep, shaky breath—in and out, in and out—which brought up an unexpected, loud hiccup. Startled, I quickly wiped my eyes and the snot dripping from my nose with the sleeve of my sweater, wincing as the rough material met my red, raw skin, leaving behind a stinging sensation. With my nose now completely stuffed up, I took a deep breath through my mouth, exhaling through gritted teeth to suppress any other involuntary sounds I might make, while feeling overwhelmed with sadness.

I wasn't stupid. I knew what death meant, but I never knew anyone who had died before. Kerrie was my first. It wasn't just that she had died, it was how she had died that was so fucking unbelievable and heartbreaking. Kerrie was gone. Forever. My heart finally accepting what my brain already knew. I would never see her pretty-cute smiling face ever again. I sniffled loudly, no longer caring about the sounds I was making, the snot, or the tears that had started up again.

As I sat crying, hugging myself, I was amazed by the steady rhythm deep within my chest, even though it felt like my heart had shattered into a million pieces.

CHAPTER 4
A MOMENTARY LAPSE OF REASON

On the eight-hour drive home from my dad's hometown, Winnipeg, Manitoba, after our summer vacations, us kids would stick our heads out the open windows or lean over the front seat to scan the treetops in search of INCO's smokestack. The only landmark nestled in the thick green northern forest that would tell us if we were almost home. No matter how road weary Dad was, he always turned it into a game, promising a quarter to the one who could spot it first.

I sat up, my back stiff and sore, searching the tops of the trees for that round, brown, ugly stack poking straight up above the treeline. When it finally appeared, I gathered my things along with the other passengers, who apparently played the game as well. With one hand resting on my backpack and the other holding on to the seat in front of me, I steadied myself as the bus bounced on the uneven road surface as it entered city limits.

When my boots touched down on the cement floor inside the bus depot, I stepped aside and out of the way of the other descending passengers to stand on my tippy toes and scan the faces of the waiting crowd. My heart fluttered when I saw Dan.

He was leaning against the wall with both hands tucked loosely in the front pockets of his jeans, cool as a cucumber, with his knee bent and one running shoe flat against the wall. He wore a black leather jacket with faded blue jeans. His sandy blond hair looked as if it had recently been washed, falling shiny and soft, past his shoulders. When our eyes met, we smiled a silent greeting at each other. I moved towards him, zigzagging through people. My smile widened, lighting up my entire face when I noticed Tammy waving madly, jumping up and down beside him.

"Hey!" I greeted them happily, dropping my heavy backpack onto the floor.

"Hey yourself." Dan smiled down at me, pushing himself away from the wall with his foot. With one hand, he took a fistful of my winter coat and pulled me to him, wrapping his arms around me and hugging me hard. I hugged him back, inhaling the smell of cigarettes, leather, and Old Spice while Tammy patted me hard on the back. It was so good to be home, I thought, reluctantly letting him go.

"I'm so sorry I didn't call you." I turned to face my best friend.

"Ah, don't worry about it. So much was going on and I knew Dan was updating you every chance he could. I was with him when he stopped at a pay phone to call you during the search." Tammy's smile wavered for a second before springing back into place. "I'm just so darn happy you're finally home!" She threw herself at me, almost knocking me over.

I held my ground, hugging her back. "Me too," I said, breathing in a mouthful of blonde hair.

"Okay, you two, let's blow this popsicle stand!" Dan said, picking up my backpack with an exaggerated groan.

Tammy and I followed Dan out to the crowded parking lot, walking arm in arm. Dan's Pontiac Parisian was parked in the middle row, still running. I slipped into the front seat, while Tammy climbed into the back, as Dan popped the trunk to drop in my backpack.

"And the world traveller returns to her hometown in ruins," a deep male voice announced from the backseat.

Startled, I turned in my seat to see Chris Jones smoking a cigarette with the window cracked open an inch. He smiled at me, showing off his straight white teeth while batting his long eyelashes surrounding his dark chocolate brown eyes. "Hey YOU! How are you?" My voice was too cheery, which didn't sound right.

Chris didn't seem to notice. "Just ducky." He took the last drag off his cigarette before flicking it out the window, almost hitting Dan. "I'm much better now that I see your pretty face." He winked at me.

Chris Jones was one of my closest and dearest "boy" friends and one of my favourite people in the entire world. The first time I ever saw him was at the beginning of the previous summer and instantly had a huge crush on him.

Last June and on the very few occasions my dad could manage a mini-family vacation that fit his meager budget, he would pack a couple coolers with food and drinks and pile us into the car at the crack of dawn to drive out to Paint Lake to rent a boat for a day of fishing. Paint Lake, a provincial park, was a thirty-minute drive south of Thompson. It was a popular resort with two public beaches, over a hundred campsites, and a huge lake littered with islands that boasted some of the best fishing spots in Northern Manitoba. The marina had a convenience store, and a restaurant/bar lounge with large windows that had a magnificent view of the blue green water. Beside the marina, and along the shoreline, was a maze of boat docks floating on top of the lake's surface. During the summer months, boat owners could rent dock spots in the floating parkade which could hold up to fifty boats of different shapes and sizes.

After a long hot day of fishing, I stood on the deck of the marina waiting for my dad to pay for the day's boat rental. Tired and sunburnt, I rested my forearms against the paint peeling railing to stare out across the lake. The sun was hovering just above the horizon, spreading the day's last beams of hazy sunlight over the calm water's surface. I squinted wearily at the scenic view as the sun's rays bounced off the lake's surface in quick flashes of light when the silhouette of a tall boy with a very odd limp caught my attention. I covered my eyes with one hand to get a better look at the teenager, who appeared to be struggling to keep his balance on the floating boardwalk. When I noticed he had two very thin and very crooked legs, I decided he wasn't drunk. With each step he took, I could tell there was a familiar rhythm to his movement, as if he had practised the walk his entire life. His right leg compensated for his left, which produced a jerking motion upward and forward, followed by a slight skip as he pulled his left leg along. When he reached the shoreline and headed towards me, I could make out his tanned boyish features. His thick messy brown hair, styled by a day out in the wind touched his neck line in waves. He was good looking, I thought to myself just as my dad came out of the store ranting about being the victim of highway robbery for the boat rental price he had to pay for just one day.

As my luck would have it, I would meet this mysterious cute boy who had caught my eye walking on the docks of Paint Lake at a party in Dan's basement weeks later. Near the end of the night, and after a few beers, I had finally worked up the nerve to plop down beside him on the couch and introduce myself. We hit it off immediately, but it wasn't long into our conversation, and to my utter disappointment, that once his dreamy chocolate brown eyes had found and focused on my tall, blond sister, he had instantly fallen in love with her.

Chris was born with spina bifida, a birth defect of the spine, which wreaked havoc on his lower limbs. Most of the time, he wore stiff plastic braces—which he absolutely hated wearing—that dug into the back of his knees to support his muscle-deprived calves. If you met him sitting down, you would never guess Chris had anything physically wrong with him. He was always happy, smart, witty, and very funny. Countless times since meeting him, he had made me laugh so hard that liquid squirted out of my nose. He took particular care in how he dressed and was obsessed with his mullet hairstyle, which he held together with large amounts of mousse and hair spray. Chris was a natural-born charmer, capable of selling a truckload of ice cubes to any Eskimo, if given the chance. When he met my strict, overbearing father for the first time, my dad instantly took a liking to this very well-mannered, polite young man, allowing Chris—the first and only teenage boy ever—to come over to the house even when Dad wasn't home. Unfortunately, Chris's good looks and charm only went so far with my older sister. Immune to his charisma, Jade made it clear from day one that she wasn't interested in dating him, ever. Chris wasn't my sister's type. Jade's boyfriends could change along with the days of the week. The boys she dated were more the strong and silent type—guys who hung on her every word—like her current boyfriend, Victor Knob, who was a quiet, short and stalky guy, who followed her around like a lost puppy dog.

"Everyone's at Nat's house right now," Dan said, pulling on his seatbelt. "I thought we would swing by there first so you could see everyone before taking you home."

"Okay," I said, "but I have to be home before Dad gets off work at four-thirty." He was working his last dayshift, which gave me a little over two hours left of freedom.

"Jade told us about Derf's lock down orders," Chris said.

Chris had given my dad the nickname Derf the first time they met. It was clever, pronouncing his name backwards, and it suited him. My father's nickname caught on quickly within the group and because it was Chris who gave it to him, my dad didn't seem to mind. In return, Derf gave Chris the nick name "Crazy Legs".

"Yeah, Derf's a little on edge," I nodded, recalling our phone conversation the night before when I told him not to worry about me getting home from the bus depot because a "friend" was going to pick me up. Lucky for me, Dad was more concerned about telling me that for the time being, Jade and I were not allowed to go anywhere unless he said so. We were expected to go straight to school and back. And if we were not home when he called from work, mark his words, he would leave work to come and find us. I knew it wasn't worth the energy to try to argue with him, because something in his tone told me there was no point. It was only after we had hung up that I figured out what that something was; it was fear. I could hear fear in my dad's voice.

"Can you blame him?" Dan snapped, shooting Chris a look through the rear-view mirror.

"Not at all." Chris held up both hands as if to protect himself from Dan's glare. "Derf's only doing what every other parent of a teenage girl should be doing in this godforsaken town right now—locking them up and throwing away the key."

"We should warn you, Kat, Natalie is pretty messed up," Tammy said, changing the subject.

"How messed up?" I asked. What does messed up look like?

"She is definitely on something," Dan said, putting the car in reverse. "I think she's taking something to calm her nerves."

Kerrie's dead and Natalie's drugged. Got it, I thought, snapping my seatbelt shut.

"It's because she feels so bloody guilty." Tammy said.

Guilty? There was no reason for Natalie to feel guilty. But I knew that was easier said than believed. I would have felt guilty too. What if it had been Tammy instead of Kerrie? I shuttered from the thought. "Are the RCMP saying anything at all?" I asked.

An odd sound came from the backseat, which made me jerk my head sideways to glance back at Chris. He had made a noise that started out as a chuckle but ended up coming out more like a cackle.

"Those idiots!" Chris declared in disgust.

I raised my eyebrows.

Dan laid an arm across the back of the front seat, cranking his neck to look over his shoulder, to back out of the narrow parking space. "They haven't said one word, not to us, anyway."

"I heard some of them puked their guts out at the scene. Goddamn rookies!" Chris ranted. "Right now, they're too busy trying to cover their asses. They refused to listen to us when we reported Kerrie missing from day one. They blew us off, then they had the balls to imply she was some sort of party girl. Then, add insult to injury, they said that she had probably just passed out somewhere or had run away. Incompetent assholes."

Chris' reaction took me by surprise. I had never seen this side of him before. Over the last few months, I had grown to love him like a big brother. I adored the charming Chris, the witty Chris, the always cracking jokes Chris. This Chris I did not know and, quiet frankly, did not want to know. "They're just doing their jobs," I offered meekly. After all, the RCMP were only human too. Not even her family or closest friends could have ever imagined something like this could have happened to Kerrie in our hometown. Why would it be any different for the RCMP?

"Yeah, right." He scoffed. "A group of us were handing out posters in the mall Friday afternoon, when one of Thompson's finest stopped us and ordered us to go home. He told us we were overreacting and that Kerrie would eventually turn up. First, they refused to file a missing persons report, and then they tried to stop us from searching for Kerrie ourselves. Can you believe that shit?" Chris asked incredulously.

I shook my head. I honestly couldn't understand why the RCMP would do that.

"Unfucking believable." Chris lit another cigarette.

"Ordering us to go home turned out to be a huge mistake because Natalie was with us," Tammy said.

"Oh?" I asked, curious, but knowing full well the force that was Natalie.

"Good ol' Nat." Chris chuckled. "She quickly told that cop off by telling him where to go and providing him clear directions on how to get there."

I smirked, easily picturing Nat with one hand on her hip, her chin raised and her brown eyes blazing; Natalie Zane was a force you just did not reckon with.

"How's everyone else doing?" I asked.

"Everybody is pretty much in shock," Dan said. "Buddy's more quiet than usual. Bruce has been rallying everyone together, and Geno, well, Geno is being Geno. He's a very angry guy at the best of times, but even more so now."

"What about Rebecca?"

"She seems to be holding her own," Dan said, "She's doing better than Natalie is, but it's hard to tell because she's always been quiet."

We drove in silence for the next few blocks, passing apartment buildings, playgrounds, and businesses that I had seen a million times before but seemed different somehow. I felt as if I was a stranger in my hometown. The sky was a gloomy dark grey, matching the mood in the car. "How did Kerrie die?" I asked.

"She was beaten to death," Dan said.

I turned my head to stare out the window, as Dan's words sunk in. Beaten to death. Beaten and death, one word violent, the other word final. Both left me feeling sick to my stomach.

"When her dad identified her body, he said she was almost unrecognizable," Chris added.

I winced, annoyed with Chris that he felt the need to add this bit of information, making my heart ache, silently wishing he hadn't.

"I've been over to the Brown's house a few times to see if they needed anything. It's a fucking scene, Katrina, I tell ya," Chris said.

I closed my eyes, picturing Mr. Brown having to identify the body of his only daughter, forced to see Kerrie like that. I couldn't imagine what that would feel like and, quite frankly, I didn't want to imagine it. And poor Mrs. Brown, who was going blind from a degenerative eye disease that I couldn't remember the name of. Her heart must be breaking over losing her little girl.

"Kerrie was raped," Dan blurted out.

I flinched and opened my eyes, from the word rape, which cast a silent spell in the car. I swallowed, worried that the egg salad sandwich would work its way back up my throat. "How—" not sure of what I wanted to ask, so I cut off my question abruptly. "Who could have? How could they? To *Kerrie?*" I shook my head and gave up, letting my questions with no answers trail off.

Dan reached over the seat to take my hand. "We're all asking the same things, Kat. This whole thing is so fucking unreal. How anyone could do that to Kerrie is hard to believe." He squeezed my hand, then let it go to once again to grip the steering wheel with white knuckles.

"We've all been wracking our brains trying to come up with who could have pulled up to Dan's house that night. Someone who might have heard about the party and tried to crash it, but came across Kerrie instead," Chris said. "All of us were there that night, the usual kids. No one was missing."

I glanced over my shoulder at him and raised an eyebrow.

He winked at me. "No one was missing that could not be accounted for," Chris corrected himself. "Nobody new showed up, which makes us all think it had to be someone we didn't know. Someone who just happened to be pulling up when Kerrie was leaving."

"And?" I asked.

Chris rolled down his window further to flick his cigarette out. "We came up with nothing. Nobody comes to mind. Natta one person."

"And it's not like Trout is on any main cruising route," Dan added. "I could understand if she was walking down Westwood Drive, then maybe someone came across her, but you have to turn onto Rainbow Crescent, then onto Trout, which is another side street."

"She would have had to walk across Westwood Drive to get to Natalie's house," Tammy interrupted.

The conversation abruptly ended when Dan turned onto Natalie's street, and we all noticed at the same time that parking was going to be a problem. There were cars lining both sides of the street. Dan found a parking spot at the end of the block. I got out and walked around to the front of the car and stood in the middle of the road. With my hands in the pockets of my coat, I stared in the direction Kerrie would have come from. She would have walked under the streetlights the entire way to Nat's house, which was halfway up the block. The time it would have taken her to get from Dan's house to Natalie's would have taken her ten minutes, tops. How could Kerrie have disappeared in such a short distance?

"You coming?" Dan stopped a few feet ahead of me.

I jammed my hands deeper into my pockets. "Yeah."

Without knocking, we walked into the Zanes' house and were greeted with the strong aroma of freshly brewed coffee. One by one, we each added our shoes to the enormous pile on the small landing and then took the two steps into the dining room attached to a small kitchen.

Mona, Natalie's mother, was standing at the sink, her hands submerged in soapy water while she stared out the kitchen window. She was an older version of her daughter, matching Natalie's height and build, but with a thicker waistline. She had short brown hair lightly sprinkled with grey. When she turned to greet us, her eyes were bloodshot and underlined with dark circles. "Hi guys." She forced a smile onto her thin lips. "There's a fresh pot of coffee if anybody wants some. Everyone is in the living room." She motioned towards the living room with her head, her hands never leaving the soapy water.

"Thanks Mona." Dan smiled at her politely.

It was impossible to make out what colour the carpet was in the living room with all the kids either sitting down or lying on it. A couch, a love seat, an old leather recliner and a square wooden, well-used coffee table sat in the middle of the small room.

"Hey Kat, I'm glad you're back." Bruce smiled up at me from the floor. He was sitting beside Rebecca, with a huge book open in front of them, turned to a page in the middle.

"Hi." I smiled at him as I reached down to squeeze Rebecca's shoulder. "Hey, Rebecca, how're you doing?"

"I'm okay," she said. With her head bowed, she reached up to pat my hand lightly with hers.

I nodded hello to Betty, who was sitting at the end of the couch. Her face was pale with pink cheeks and puffy red eyes. Her usually wild hair style was tamed, falling straight and limp around her sad features. I offered a warm smile at Janis, who was sitting on the floor by Geno's feet, his massive frame filling up the leather recliner in the corner of the room. When I saw Natalie, my breath caught in my throat. She was sitting at the end of the larger couch, her long brown hair a matted mess, pulled loose into a bun and piled on top of her head. Stray strands stuck out angrily and surrounded her pale face. She was as white as a ghost. Both of her knees were pulled up close to her chest, with her arms wrapped tightly around them. There were dark circles under both her eyes, which also matched her mother's. She was staring straight ahead, her face expressionless and blank, as if she were in some sort of trance.

I carefully stepped over kids to get to her, not sure of what I was going to say, but feeling drawn to her just the same. When I stood in front of her, I knelt and gently placed both my hands on her arms, scared I was going to startle her. She didn't even flinch.

"Hey, Nat," I whispered softly.

Natalie deliberately turned her head to gaze down at me.

I fought back tears when our eyes meet, the pain, grief and sadness emanating off her was so overpowering it took my breath away.

"Hey, you're back." Her voice was hoarse and just above a whisper.

"Yeah, I just got back. I'm so, so sorry, Nat," I said, gently squeezing her arms.

That fiery spark I had witnessed, so many times, in Natalie's eyes was now gone, replaced with pure pain. I had never seen anyone so heartbreakingly sad in my entire life.

She nodded once before slipping back into her grief to stare straight ahead, blinking at nothing at all.

Buddy, who was sitting beside her, got up and motioned for me to take his spot.

I nodded my thanks at him and sank into the brown couch with dusty rose flowers scattered all over it.

A low hum of muffled voices filled the room as Bruce and Rebecca flipped through the pages of that huge book with the golden edges, to stop and point at something on the page while they nodded at each other. Then Rebecca would write something down in a notebook that lay on her lap. The book was the biggest Bible I had ever seen.

"What are they doing?" I whispered to Tammy, who had managed to squeeze in on the other side of me.

"They're picking Bible verses to read at Kerrie's funeral," Tammy whispered back.

Kerrie's funeral? Of course, there was going to be a funeral. How was I just realizing this now? I had never been to a funeral before. "When is it?" I asked.

"Wednesday," Tammy replied.

The atmosphere in the room felt wrong. It was an overwhelming feeling of grief that matched the sullen and drawn expressions on everyone's faces. It just didn't feel right. The air was thick with sadness, almost suffocating. These were the same kids I had hung out with, laughed with, sang with, and guzzled my first beer with, and now they all had the same grief ridden looks on their faces, while watching Rebecca and Bruce choose the "right" verse from a Bible that would represent what we were all feeling and the biblical lesson to be learned from our friend's murder. Did such a verse exist? I didn't know—or hadn't thought about if any of us even went to church or were even religious, for that matter.

"Coffee's ready if anyone wants some." Mona poked her head into the doorway of the living room.

I grabbed Tammy's hand and stood up, pulling her with me, seeing a chance for a quick escape, when a strange noise stopped us in our tracks.

Geno was leaning forward, both his elbows on his knees, with his sausage-thick fingers covering his face as his whole body shook violently. It took me a second to understand what he was doing. When I did, I was shocked. Geno was crying. Not just crying—he was sobbing uncontrollably. Big, strong, built-like-a-brick-shithouse Geno was crying like a baby. Janis scooted her bum across the floor to place a hand on his arm while Bruce got up and stood in front of him. He took hold of both of Geno's massive shoulders, trying to steady the oversized man-child, who was now shaking his head from side to side.

"Oh my god, who could have done this to Kerrie!?" Geno's desperate question was muffled by his massive hands.

Bruce leaned down to whisper something in his ear, which only made Geno cry even louder.

That did it. I moved quickly, hop scotching over kids dragging Tammy with me. In the kitchen, Dan was leaning casually up against the counter, holding a fresh cup of coffee.

"Can we go?" I asked.

He glanced down at me, confused.

"Please?" I pleaded through gritted teeth.

He nodded, then dumped his full cup of coffee down the sink. "Thanks for the coffee, Mona, but I think we're going to take off now."

Mona hugged each of us while we took turns putting on our shoes. "You kids take care of yourselves. Remember you're always welcome here." Her smile didn't reach her tired eyes.

Outside, I took huge gulps of the fresh air as we walked down the driveway.

"What the hell guys!? You were just going to leave me here!?" Chris yelled after us.

We all stopped and turned around to see Chris teetering on the top of the steps. He was trying to keep his balance while pulling on his red and black flannel lumber jacket.

I retraced my footsteps up the driveway to climb the four stairs to take his arm, helping him down.

"Sorry. I just couldn't stay in that house any longer," I explained, letting go of his arm once I was sure both of his twisted feet were on solid ground.

"I hear ya! Seeing the big guy cry was weird as shit." Chris shook his head. "Who knew Geno had a heart, let alone the tears, to go along with it? Hard to see a grown ass man-child cry."

I laughed out loud and immediately felt guilty for it.

"Where to?" Dan asked once we were back in the car and buckled up.

"Can we just cruise around for a bit?" I asked.

Dan nodded, pulling away from the curve.

"Poor Mona," Chris sighed. "She looks like she's been beating herself up about Kerrie."

"Why?" I asked.

"Because she didn't listen when Nat told her that Kerrie had disappeared," Chris said.

I totally got why Mona would feel guilty, but seriously, how was she supposed to know? How could anyone know that this could have happened to Kerrie?

Dan slowed the car down while driving over a deep dip on Westwood drive.

"I just can't wrap my brain around Kerrie being dead," Chris blurted out. "That she is really fucking gone, and that we're never going to see her again. Ever."

"I know," Tammy agreed. "I was talking to her at the party that night. She was happy and bubbly, the same old Kerrie, just sweet. It doesn't feel like she's actually gone to me, either."

We were at the end of Westwood Drive, stopped at the red light. Dan flipped the signal light to go left onto Thompson Drive.

This was the route Kerrie would have taken, I thought, staring up at the red light.

"On Friday night, after searching for Kerrie all afternoon, I had to go to work," Chris said. He worked part-time as a disc jockey at the CHTM radio station. "I couldn't focus. I would announce the next song, begin to play said song, and something inside me would say, 'Nope, that is not the right song.'

I would then stop the song right in the middle and change it to something else. Rinse and repeat."

Sometimes, when Dan was working at his part-time job delivering pizzas for Santa Maria, I would get him to drop me off at the radio station to hang out with Chris to keep him company. I would browse through the radio station's massive music library, or pull records for him, or just sit beside him in the control booth with my feet up, threatening to push random buttons with my big toe.

Once, when Chris was announcing the top of the hour news from a piece of paper torn from the news prompter, I stood in front of him making silly faces, trying to make him laugh. He would only have to raise the paper a few inches upward to block out my silliness, which left me no other choice but to light the thin paper he was holding on fire with my lighter. It was a true test of his focus while speaking live on the air, which he, of course, passed with flying colours. His deep voice remained steady as he continued to read, as he licked his fingertips between sentences, then calmly snuffing out the flame creeping up from the bottom of the page.

"It sounds like you had a momentary lapse of reason." Dan raised an eyebrow, studying Chris in the rear-view mirror.

"BINGO! That's it! A momentary lapse of reason!" Chris slapped his boney knee hard.

I rolled my eyes. Dan and Chris were always coming up with weird explanations for things. They were both creatively smart, and would sit for hours in Chicken Chef debating or discussing useless topics like what were the risks of dying if one would parachute off the Burntwood bridge? What amount of physical strength would it take if that parachute happened to fail to beat the currents raging underneath the choppy river's surface? What would be the formula needed to survive such an encounter? The powerful force of the river versus the human strength to conquer it?

"I like it! Nail on the head, my friend, nail on the head. That's exactly what I had, a momentary lapse of reason." Chris repeated the words slowly, as if tasting them. "Only I had a million momentary lapses of reasons during that eight-hour shift." He shook his head. "I wish you were there, kiddo, could have kept me a little sane." Chris smiled at me.

"I wish I was there, too." I smiled back.

"Did anyone complain?" Tammy asked.

"Don't know. Don't care." Chris shrugged.

We slid to a stop at the next icy intersection.

"Turn left," I said without thinking.

"Are you sure?" Dan asked.

"Yeah." I sounded braver than I felt. "I just want to drive out to where she was found." I turned in my seat. "Is that okay?"

Both Tammy and Chris nodded.

"There still might be cops everywhere," Tammy said.

"Fuck 'em. It's not illegal to drive down a public highway," Chris said.

When the light turned green, Dan turned the car towards the Burntwood bridge.

I closed my eyes as we crossed over the raised seam that separated the bridge from the road. Without looking—I had crossed the bridge a million times—I knew the water below was moving fast and furious, with large white swells. When I felt the car drive over the seam to get back on the highway, I took a deep, shaky breath in before opening my eyes, the car now passing Popeyes, a seasonal burger joint, boarded up and closed for the winter.

My heart picked up speed when Dan gently stepped on the brake to slow the car down to make the left turn onto the stable road. The clicking of the turn signal was the only sound in the car. As the tires touched the gravel road, my heart suddenly felt like it was going to explode in my chest. Images of Kerrie swam before my eyes—quick, brief, horrific flashes. Kerrie being dragged into a car. Kerrie being held down. Kerrie being beaten. Then Kerrie's body being dropped onto the cold, hard ground, left all by herself in the woods, Kerrie lying motionless.

I was now hyper-ventilating and desperately trying to catch my breath. I leaned forward in my seat to grab onto the dash with both hands, trying to suck air into my lungs. "Please! Don't go any further," I managed between gasps, my face covered in sweat, only seeing black spots in front of me.

Dan quickly pulled the car over to the side of the road. "Katrina? What's wrong? Are you okay?" He put a hand on my shoulder.

I shook my head. "I changed my mind. Please. Turn around." My eyes squeezed shut. "Please," I begged.

I could hear Tammy take off her seatbelt, then felt her hand on my back. "It's okay Katrina, just breathe."

"I think you need to listen to your lady." Chris' deep voice came from somewhere far off in the distance.

"Okay." Dan slammed the car back into drive. "Any cars coming?"

"You're clear here," Chris said.

When I felt the car make a U-turn, I became dizzy and gritted my teeth, swallowing hard while praying. *Don't puke! Don't puke! Please don't puke in front of your boyfriend and in his car!* I kept repeating this over and over in my head as I felt Dan slam his foot on the gas pedal, sending rocks flying behind us as he sped back down the dirt road. When the car was back on the highway, my heart slowed, and my lungs opened just as we crossed back over the bridge. After a couple of deep breaths, I opened my eyes.

"God, I'm so sorry," I whispered, embarrassed. I leaned back in my seat. Whatever it was, it was gone now. My heart was beating normally again.

"It's okay," Tammy patted my shoulder before sitting back to put her seatbelt on.

"Better?" Dan glanced over at me out of the corner of his eye.

"Much." I nodded. "It came on all of a sudden. I just couldn't breathe the minute we turned onto the stable road. I'm so sorry." I felt so stupid. "Nothing like that has ever happened to me before."

Dan reached over to grab my hand. "Don't worry about it. As long as you're okay now?"

"I think so." I forced a smile.

"Don't sweat it, beautiful," Chris said, lighting another cigarette. "It was just one of those momentary lapses in reason."

***

An hour later, Dan and I were parked in my driveway after we had dropped off Chris and Tammy at their homes. I stared at the Gingerbread House through the windshield. It felt so good to be home.

Dan took his seatbelt off and turned in his seat to face me. "Hi." He smiled.

"Hi" I smiled back.

He leaned over and kissed me gently on the lips.

I kissed him back.

When he pulled away from me, I moved to sit right next to him and leaned in. He wrapped his arms around me.

"What happened to you back there?" he asked, his chin resting on the top of my head.

"I don't know. The minute we turned onto the stable road, I imagined what Kerrie must have gone through that night. I could actually feel it. It suddenly felt just too. . ." I searched my brain, trying to think of the right word.

"Real?" he finished for me.

"Yeah, too real," I agreed. "I'm sorry."

"You have nothing to be sorry about. What happened to her has been a little too real for all of us."

I nodded. Poor sweet Kerrie. She did not deserve what happened to her. I squeezed my eyes shut, feeling the tears once again starting to come.

"You know what I can't stop thinking about?" Dan gently pushed me away from him, putting me at arm's length.

"What?" I asked, disappointed at the space he had created between us.

"That it could have been you," he whispered.

I scrunched up my face. Me? That thought had never even crossed my mind. How could it have been me?

"I've been secretly thanking God you weren't at my house that night. You could have walked home by yourself. You'd done it before, and I would have let you without giving it a second thought." His words caught in his throat.

I shook my head. "But it wasn't me. And it shouldn't have been Kerrie either." I reached up to put my hands on both his cheeks.

"I know," he said. "But I can't help but feel guilty."

"Guilty? About what? You have nothing to feel guilty about. Because you had a party that night? That's what kids do, that's what *we* do. What happened to Kerrie is nobody's fault. Not Kerrie's, not Chad's, not Natalie's, and not anyone's. It's whoever did this to her. That is whose fault it is. No one else. Okay?"

He took a deep shaky breath in. "Promise me that from now on you will not walk anywhere, especially by yourself. If you need a ride, you call me. Any time, day or night, I will come get you and drive you wherever you want to go."

"Okay." I bit my bottom lip, knowing I was lying to him. Because I had made the exact opposite promise to my dad. I was forbidden to even be in a vehicle with a boy, day or night. Dan had heard that Derf could be overprotective when it came to his teenage daughters but he had no idea he had already broken a major rule in our house, by dating me.

"I mean it, Kat," Dan said, misreading my expression. "It's not safe."

"Ah, that might be a problem," I said, dropping my hands in my lap and bowing my head.

"Why?"

"I'm actually not allowed to date anyone until I'm sixteen," I confessed.

Dan put a finger under my chin and raised it. When our eyes meet, I held my breath.

"So, Derf doesn't know about me, or about us?" He didn't sound the least bit surprised.

I shook my head.

Dan turned in his seat and put the car in reverse. "Well, we're going to have to change that," he said, backing out of the driveway.

"Wait! What are you doing?"

"Better late than never, Katrina. Derf's going to find out about us, eventually," he pulled the car alongside the curb in front of the house, shut it off and got out of the car.

"Yeah but. . ." I clambered out my door. "Dan, I don't think now is the right time," I stammered, standing on the curb watching him open the trunk to get my backpack then slam it shut.

He shoved the car keys into his jacket pocket. "Trust me," he walked around the front of the car, and stopped to hold out his hand.

I reluctantly took it.

"Hey sis!" Jade greeted us from the kitchen as Dan and I walked through the front door.

I took my backpack from him and motioned for him to sit on the couch. My brother was in his usual spot, lying on the floor in front of the TV.

"Hey bud, whatcha watching?" Dan asked my little brother.

I went to my room to toss my backpack on my unmade bed.

"What's going on?" I heard my sister ask, clearly surprised to see Dan sitting on our couch.

"I'm finally going to meet Derf," Dan replied cheerfully.

Jade was standing in the middle of the living room, holding a tea towel. "Whoa! Seriously? I wouldn't have guessed you had the balls." She turned as I came back into the room. "And you think this is a good idea?" she asked, her green eyes wide.

Right on cue, I could hear Dad's car a few blocks away, the loud muffler announcing his impending arrival.

I shrugged. "I have no idea," I mumbled just as our father's car passed the bay window and turned sharply into our driveway—right on schedule.

"Oh my god, this is going to be good!" Jade flipped the tea towel over her shoulder and crossed her arms.

My brother continued to watch TV, oblivious to what was going on around him.

My father's heavy work boots echoed on the front porch steps and throughout the entire house. When Dad opened the front door, my sister bolted to greet him just as he stepped into the foyer.

"Hey Dad! Let me take those from you." She took the two bags of groceries and his lunch pail from him, freeing up both his hands.

"Did your sister make it home?" He stepped into the living room, then stopped short when he saw Dan sitting in his favourite spot on the couch.

On cue, Dan jumped up and held out his hand. "Hi, Mr. McGane. I'm Dan Safflower, a friend of your daughters."

My father looked Dan up and down, before setting his mouth into a straight line. They were almost the same height—almost. Dan was a few inches shorter, but my dad was a lot wider. After a suspenseful moment of silence, Dad finally took Dan's hand and gripped it in a firm handshake. "Good to meet you," he said, his tone oddly too polite.

I started to breathe again.

"I just wanted to introduce myself to you because Katrina needed a ride home from the bus depot today, and given everything that's going on right now, I thought it would be a good idea that you know who your daughters are hanging out with." Dan's voice was steady as a rock.

I was impressed. My sister was not. Out of the corner of my eye I could see the disappointment on Jade's face after she had come back into the living room to find my boyfriend holding his own with our father.

I watched as the expression on our dad's face change from suspicion to understanding why a strange teenage boy was now standing in the middle of his living room.

"I also wanted to let you know I'm available to drive both your daughters around, if and when they need a ride." Dan quickly added.

"That's a very generous offer young man but I'll have to think about it," my dad replied gruffly.

"Okay." Dan nodded then turned to me, then Jade. "Well, I should be going."

"Jade, come help me put away these groceries," Dad said heading to the kitchen. "Jake, move away from that goddamn TV!" he barked over his shoulder.

My brother was always sitting too close to the television set. On command, Jake scooted his butt back a foot without taking his eyes off the program he was watching.

I crossed my arms in front of my chest and leaned against the doorframe of the foyer, watching as Dan put his sneakers back on.

"I'll phone you later," he said, standing up, shaking his leather jacket back into place.

"Sure." I smiled. "I'm impressed, by the way, and I think Dad was too."

"Mission accomplished." He winked before disappearing through the front door.

Jade was already starting in on Dad when I walked into the kitchen.

"So, Katrina's allowed to bring a boy home, and that's okay?" my sister asked in utter disbelief.

My father's huge presence made my sister look small in comparison. I noticed for the first time that the role of being a single father was wearing on his patience—patience that was stretched to it limits when having to deal with the drama of his teenage daughters. Add to that, our father had a very short fuse because of his Irish Temper—or IT, as Jade and I called it. Dad's IT, when unleashed, was to say the least, intimidating. His IT could go off at any time with the simple flip of an emotional switch, a switch that my sister would flip "on" as often as she could.

"Glad you're home safe, baby girl," Dad said, ignoring my sister's recent accusation of unfairness.

Jade stood as tall as she could with her arms crossed in front of her impressive chest and with one hip jutted out, her normal battle stance, watching as my dad unpacked the groceries. This was Jade's idea of helping put the groceries away. "Dad?!"

"I let you bring a boy home." Dad slammed a cupboard door shut. "What about Crazy Legs?"

"Oh my god! He's not my boyfriend! He's Kat's friend." She threw her hands up in the air.

Dad shot her a disbelieving look over his shoulder.

So, our dad could see it too. Chris' unrequited love for my sister.

"You girls will not be *going out* with anyone, boys or girls for the time being. You both are to come straight home from school, do your chores, and take care of your brother." He put a colander in the sink and dropped a head of iceberg lettuce in it before turning on the cold water on full blast.

"That's so not fair!" my sister screeched in protest.

I sat down at the kitchen table, knowing it was best to say nothing. Before Kerrie's murder, we were allowed to go out twice a week on school nights. This depended, of course, on if our chores were done and our grades were good. Chores that were always written out in dad's messy handwriting on a pad of paper left daily on the kitchen table. My dad was famous for lists—chore lists, grocery lists, and reminder lists.

"Its non-negotiable. For now, both of you are to be at home every night especially when I'm at work, so I know you're both safe," he opened the fridge door.

"This is such bullshit," my sister mumbled.

Switch flipped.

"Watch your mouth, young lady!" Dad turned to glare at my sister. "You both are on lock down until further notice. I start afternoons this week, and if either of you are not at home to answer the phone when I call, there will be hell to pay. Mark my words."

"You can't be serious?" Jade was far from giving up. "You *are* grounding us? For doing *nothing*? How is that fair? What happened to Kerrie wasn't our fault. We need to be with our friends right now."

He shut the fridge door, holding a loaf tin which I was guessing was a meatloaf. "I DON'T want either of you walking the streets right now! A girl in town was just murdered. WHAT DON'T YOU UNDERSTAND?" He gaped at me and then back at Jade, his brown eyes wide. The lines around his eyes were a bit deeper, his hair a bit greyer. He shook his head before he wrenched the oven door open to throw the brick of meat on the middle rack and then slammed the oven door shut and turned the dial.

"Not just a girl, Dad," I said, "Kerrie was our friend."

"Now she speaks!" my sister snapped, shooting me a look.

Dad raised both his hands in the air. "Jesus Christ! Don't you think I know that?" His hands moved to cover his face as he shook his head back and forth. After rubbing his face hard, he dropped his hands back down by his sides. "Did I ever meet her?" His voice lowered, his IT calming.

"No." Jade and I answered him together.

Kerrie had been at the house a few times, coming to a couple of our parties over the summer. She had stood in the kitchen, cheering on Geno, while he chugged a beer attached to a funnel in the exact spot dad was standing in right now.

"I didn't think so," he shut the water off. Then rested both hands on the counter and stare out the window over the sink. "I can't imagine what her parents are going through right now. AND selfishly I don't want to. I AM your father, AND because I am your father, what I say goes. END OF DISCUSSION." He turned to give Jade a look that meant business.

"What about my job?" my sister asked.

"If you have to work, then you go straight to work and come straight home." He reached for a knife from the wooden block by the stove.

"What about school?" she asked.

I frowned, wondering where she was going with this.

"What about it?" My father shook the head of lettuce a little too roughly which made water fly everywhere, before dropping it on the cutting board.

"How are we getting to school? Are you going to drive us every day?" My sister knew this was impossible with his work schedule. She was flicking the IT back on. "How are we supposed to stay off the streets? Seriously, Dad? What you're saying doesn't make any sense."

My father stopped, the knife hovering over the head of lettuce, his cheeks turning a bright red.

"Dan did offer to drive us if we needed him to," I jumped in, seeing the door of opportunity open and diving right through it.

"And we have other friends that could drive us around too," my sister chimed in.

"What other friends?" Dad asked, chopping up the lettuce loudly.

"Dan, Buddy, Victor, and Bruce," Jade said.

"All boys," my dad said under his breath more to himself, as he scooped up the leafy green pieces to drop them into a bowl.

"Friends," my sister insisted. "Boys with cars that are *just* friends."

"Any boy you plan on getting into a car with, I will meet first," he said, sounding defeated.

"Fine," my sister said, "and on week nights—"

"You both are to be home."

She glared at him, her lips set into that familiar straight line.

"Not another word, young lady. I mean it," he warned, his knife not missing a beat while he chopped up a helpless carrot.

My sister let out a dramatic scream before storming out of the kitchen.

"Do you have anything you would like to add?" He stopped to point the knife in my direction.

"Nope." I got up from the table to follow my sister's lead, only quietly.

"HE'S being so UNFAIR!" my sister cried when I entered our room. She was lying on her bed glaring up at the ceiling.

I shut our bedroom door and pushed my backpack off my bed before crawling onto it. Our beds were positioned against two walls in an L-shape. Where my head was, her feet were right beside it. My dad built our beds with his bare hands making the bed frames from cut down spruce trees that he had stripped off the bark, sanded down then treated with varnish until the logs were shiny and smooth. The beds matched the overall décor of the Gingerbread House perfectly.

"Aren't you even a little pissed at him?" Jade asked.

"He's scared Jade, that's all." I sighed, rolling on my side and away from her feet to face the wall, feeling exhausted. The last two days had been draining, and I had a feeling the next few days were going to be even worse.

***

After supper, I called Dan to fill him in on my dad's new rules, and he took my house arrest in stride. Before hanging up, he promised to pick us up for school the next morning. For the rest of the night, I hung out in my bedroom, listening to music and writing in my journal, trying not to listen to my sister talk for hours on the phone to whoever would listen about how unfair and crazy our father was.

The next morning, I got up as if it was any other normal school day. While I was stuffing my books into by book bag, Jade came into our bedroom, her hair still wet and wrapped in a towel.

I was instantly ticked off. Jade never helped with getting Jake ready in the mornings and always crawled out of bed at the last minute. "You better hurry up if you want a ride to school. Dan is going to be here any minute."

When I got into Dan's car, I slammed the door shut. "Jade should be out in a minute." I didn't try to hide my irritation as I reached for my seatbelt.

"No problem." Dan put the car back into park. "We're not going to school, anyway."

"What? Where are we going?"

"I'm pretty sure our teachers aren't expecting us in class this week, so I thought we could all just hang out at my place. My parents will both be at work, and they said it would be okay." He reached over to take my hand and kissed it.

"So, we won't get marked absent?" That was all I needed, to get in trouble with Dad for skipping school in the state he was already in.

"Probably not, but do you really feel like going to school?"

"No," I said, but truthfully, I didn't know what I was feeling. Life as we knew it had turned completely upside down.

Jade got into the backseat, clutching her purse and a notebook that had seen better days. Her hair was still wet. "Okay, let's roll!" She reached for her seat belt.

"Apparently, we're not going to school," I informed her.

"Cool," she said.

That day and the next, when the bell rang at 9:00 a.m. throughout the halls of RD Parker High School, all of Kerrie's friends gathered in the basement on Trout Ave. We spent the school hours of the day smoking cigarettes, drinking pots of coffee and when the basement walls started to close in, we ventured out to either cruise around the streets aimlessly or go to Chicken Chef for fries and gravy. We talked, we laughed, we cried, we watched movies, we played cards, and we listened to music while trying to prepare ourselves for Kerrie's funeral on Wednesday. It was comforting to be around people who knew her and who were riding the same roller coaster of emotions. We were all snapped in on the same unpredictable ride, with the looping and winding of emotions of grief, each of us holding on while trying to come to terms with the fact that Kerrie was truly gone.

At times it felt like we were all in our very own private group therapy session. Discussing, at length and in detail various scenarios of what could have happened to Kerrie that night. We went over and over the events leading up to her disappearance while trying to nail down the timeline and, of course, possible suspects. But there wasn't one person we could think of that could be capable of doing what was done to Kerrie. Wherever our group conversation travelled, we always came back around to that one question that weighed on our minds—would Kerrie have gotten into a car with someone she didn't know? Most of us couldn't see her doing that. We wondered why would Kerrie want a ride, when she was supposed to sleep at Natalie's that night? If Kerrie *was* drunk, possibly sick, making her want to sleep in her own bed and thankful for the offer of a ride home? But everyone who had been at the party swore that Kerrie didn't seem drunk, just upset after Chad had arrived. We circled around this topic, over and over again.

During those two days, one by one, different kids who had attended the party were called in by the lead investigator on the case, Constable Crostini requesting their presence at the local RCMP detachment downtown for questioning. Bruce was one of the first to go, followed by Geno, then Chris, then Buddy, and so on.

When Buddy reappeared in the basement following hours of questioning, he was paler than usual. He sat on the couch and after lighting a cigarette, said nothing for the longest time.

"How'd it go?" Dan finally asked, after Buddy stubbed out his cigarette in the overflowing ashtray.

"Brutal." He sighed, shaking his head.

"What do you mean, brutal?" I asked.

"They questioned me for over two hours. Asking the same thing over and over, as if they were trying to trip me up or something. Halfway through, I started to think I was a suspect."

"What!?" Rebecca asked surprised.

Buddy rubbed the stubble on his chin with one hand. "They seemed to be super focused on my parent's car."

"Your car?" Bruce asked. "What about it?"

"Whether the car was mine or not. Who in my family drove it? How often was I given permission to drive it? Where was my family the night of the murder? How many times was Kerrie in it." He shrugged.

I blinked away the image of Kerrie's smiling face peeking up and over the front seat of Buddy's car during one of our Car Tag nights.

"They're focusing on us, because they have no leads. Go figure," Chris said in disgust, shaking his head.

"Wouldn't you focus on us first, if you were the police?" Dan asked. "All the guys in this room should be questioned, if for no other reason but to rule us out. Which only means that they are doing their jobs."

Dan got up from the recliner to go and sit beside Buddy on the couch. He placed one hand on his shoulder. "Hey man, don't sweat it."

Everyone murmured in agreement.

"Did they ask you about *your car*?" Chris asked Bruce.

"No." He shook his head. "They asked about the kids in our group. They did ask a lot of questions about Chad, though. Like, how long Kerrie and he dated, and what type of guy he was."

We hadn't seen or heard from Chad since Kerrie's murder, which none of us thought suspicious because Chad rarely hung around with us even before he started dating Kerrie. He was most likely keeping his distance because he also felt guilty for being the reason Kerrie wanted to leave the party in the first place. We all believed that Chad was a good guy, a decent guy, and would never intentionally hurt Kerrie.

My heart went out to all the guys, as I glanced around the basement, briefly studying each one of their faces. They all wore the same strained expression—a mixture of grief and confusion. Grieving Kerrie was one thing; having to prove that they had nothing to do with her murder was an entirely different thing. I knew with all my heart that not one of them was capable of doing what was done to Kerrie, I was absolutely sure of it—well, my heart was, anyway.

CHAPTER 5
SHE LEFT A BEAUTIFUL MEMORY

I woke up Wednesday morning with the sound of the October wind howling outside my bedroom window. My first thought when rolling over was that today was Kerrie's funeral.

The last two days had been physically draining. Each day, I came home "after school" to fall into bed shortly after supper emotionally exhausted. In the basement on Trout Ave, each one of us, at some point, came to terms with our grief through either an all-out meltdown, an outburst of anger, or by sitting alone in the corner, wiping away silent tears. We took turns consoling one another, calming the person down, or soothing them when it finally "hit" them that Kerrie was gone. It felt like we were all trapped inside a suffocating bubble of grief.

Selfishly, I wanted to pop that bubble, then felt guilty for even thinking it. Whatever I was feeling was nothing compared to what Kerrie's family was going through, especially today, when they had to say their final goodbyes to their only daughter and sister.

"Are you girls up yet?" Dad burst through our bedroom door to stand in the middle of our messy room while drying his hands on a tea towel.

My sister was right. Some days, my dad was like a bull let loose in a China shop.

"Yeah." I blinked up at him.

"Do you have to yell?" my sister groaned, slamming her pillow over her head.

"I'm making French toast for breakfast. Do you girls need a ride to the church?"

"No. Dan's picking us up," I threw off my heavy quilt and stretched.

"Okay, breakfast will be ready in ten minutes." He scanned our messy bedroom disapprovingly but said nothing, then leaving just as he had come in.

"Are you going to shower?" I asked Jade's feet poking out from under her quilt.

"What time will Dan be here?" Her question was muffled from the pillow still over her head.

"Eight-thirty."

Everyone was supposed to meet in the church's basement an hour before the service. Bruce and Rebecca had helped Kerrie's parents organize the entire funeral. I had no idea what to expect. I only knew Natalie was going to do Kerrie's eulogy.

"I'll go shower first." I climbed out of bed.

Thirty minutes later, Jade and I were bumping into each other while trying to get ready.

"Have you seen my navy-blue blazer with the shoulder pads?" I was standing in front of our closet scanning the clutter of unorganized hanging clothes.

"Nope," Jade replied.

"I'm sure I just saw it the other day," I muttered more to myself, flipping through the hangers. Finally giving up, I decide on my black blazer with the shoulder pads instead, with a white blouse and black stirrup pants.

After putting on makeup, I stepped back from our makeshift make-up vanity, which was the top of our shared six drawer wooden dresser with a large mirror, for one last look.

"Is that what you're wearing?" Jade asked, her hair in a towel twist while she buttoned up a black blouse.

"What's wrong with it?" I turned back to face the mirror. My brown hair was brushed shiny and fell loose past my shoulders, my bangs split down the middle and feathered. My outfit was mostly black, which seemed right for a funeral. Aren't you supposed to wear black to a funeral?

"I'm only teasing you. You look fine." Jade shook her head and shoved me out of the way to pick up the blow dryer.

Jade had chosen a jean skirt, its hem brushed just past her kneecaps, with black leggings that matched her black blouse.

I left her to blow dry her long thin blonde hair, which I knew, from waiting for her a million times, would take exactly four minutes.

Dad was sitting at the kitchen table, smoking a cigarette and drinking coffee. "Your plate is in the oven," he said. "You look nice, baby girl."

"Thanks." I went to the stove and slipped on an oven mitt.

"Are you sure you don't want me to come with you girls?" he asked for the hundredth time.

"I'm sure," I put the warm plate with two thick slices of French toast on the table beside him. My dad was a great cook, and his French toast was one of our favourite breakfasts.

There were two reasons Jade and I insisted Dad should not come with us to Kerrie's funeral. The first was that he never met Kerrie. The second, and more importantly, was that we were scared the funeral might set him off again, spiralling him back into that panic of parental protection and adding more or extending the rules to our current lockdown status. He was starting his afternoon shift rotation the next day, which would give us some freedom and a much-needed break from his overbearing presence in the house.

When Dan walked into the kitchen thirty minutes later, Jade and I were putting our breakfast dishes in the dishwasher. He looked handsome, wearing black dress pants and a white dress shirt with a black tie that matched his black leather jacket.

"Hi, Mr. McGane," Dan greeted Dad politely.

Dad nodded and got up from the table. "I need to go check on your brother."

"You two look nice," Dan said, when he was sure Derf was out of earshot.

"Thanks!" My sister smiled up at him. "Can we pick up Vic on the way?"

"Okay." Dan glanced up at the clock. "But we better get going."

Fifteen minutes later, Dan pulled into the crowded parking lot at the St. Lawrence Church just before nine. When we got out of the car, the bone chilling October wind forced us to keep our heads down as we walked across the icy parking lot to the side entrance. I followed Dan down a narrow stairwell that led to the basement and into a large room filled with empty tables. Together, we all moved towards the sound of voices coming from the kitchen on the far side of the room.

Dan took my coat and went to find a place to hang it up as I glanced around the crowded kitchen. Everyone was dressed in their Sunday best, and there was a low murmur of nervous chatter that filled the small room.

"Hey, beautiful." Chris appeared beside me, casually draping an arm across my shoulders.

"Hey." I looked him up and down and whistled softly. "You clean up nice, my friend." I smiled.

He was wearing a black dress shirt with matching dress pants that had recently been pressed. The sharp crease ran down the middle of both legs. As usual, the bottom cuffs of his pants were tucked neatly into thick, grey wool socks. He wore his bright white high-top sneakers, meant to provide some support to his weak ankles. He had obviously decided against wearing his leg braces.

"Thanks for noticing. Now, where is that gorgeous sister of yours?" Chris squinted, moving his head back and forth to scan the crowded room.

"Over there." I nodded in Jade's direction. She was talking to Janis, Betty, and Tammy.

"Hot damn," he muttered under his breath.

"Would you quit it?" I nudged him hard in the ribs. "We're at a funeral."

Jade's complete lack of interest in Chris was for the best. I had no desire to guide one of my dearest friends through the never-ending storm that was my sister. After all, Victor was the perfect guy for her. He was quiet and content with being in her shadow as my sister demanded the spotlight. Victor reminded me of one of those trained obedience dogs that follow their owners mindlessly around everywhere.

"Your poor misguided sister." Chris shook his head. "What does she see in him?"

"Victor is a nice enough guy," I said for the thousandth time.

"Well, you know what they say about nice guys finishing last?" Chris dropped his arm from my shoulders and stood up, making himself as tall as his legs would allow before doing his best to walk straight and confidently toward my unsuspecting sister.

I rolled my eyes, watching as Chris cleverly inserted himself between Jade and Victor, pushing her boyfriend deeper into the shadows.

"Hey, the church is packed solid." Dan leaned down to whisper in my ear. "It looks like the entire city is up there."

"Seriously? Where are we going to sit?" I asked.

"Don't worry, I think that there are seats reserved for us."

"Hey, you two." Brad Fuller strolled over to stand beside Dan. He looked extremely uncomfortable in his dark grey dress pants with a crisp white dress shirt and matching dark grey tie. Brad's family had moved to Thompson from Newfoundland a few years back. His sharp eastern accent was a dead give away. He was a short, stalky guy with brown, wavy hair and matching brown eyes. Brad scowled as he tugged on the knot of his tie which was pressing up against his Adam's apple.

"Hey, where's Laura?" I asked him.

Brad and Laura had been a couple for as long as I had been a part of the group, and they were made for each other. Laura was a spunky girl with fair skin and thick, curly brown hair. Brad had a reputation for being very opinionated and, at times, even vulgar, for which he was always excused because of his Newfoundland heritage. After witnessing Laura put Brad in his place a few times, it became obvious right away—at least to me—that they were meant for each other.

"Over there." He nodded towards a group of girls standing with my sister. "Gabbing away as per usual." He again pulled at the knot of his tie.

As if she had heard him, Laura separated herself from the girls to stand beside him.

"Hey, Laura." I eyed up her navy-blue blazer with shoulder pads.

"Hey, Kat." She smiled at me. "You look nice."

"Thanks. So do you. Where did you get the nice blazer?" I had to ask.

"Oh, your sister sold it to me for twenty bucks yesterday when I told her I had nothing to wear to the funeral." She stretched both her arms out to admire it.

I forced a smile and nodded, then shot my sister a dirty look. As if I had reached across the room and tapped Jade on the shoulder, she glanced over at me, then turned her back, entwining one arm with Victor, who had managed to position himself beside her again.

"Okay everyone, can I please have your attention?!" Bruce yelled over the slow growing noise of nervous chatter. He was standing in the middle of the kitchen smartly dressed in a three-piece black business suit with a white shirt and a red tie.

After a minute of loud shushing, the room finally fell silent.

"Everybody is going to be pairing up and getting into one line. The person on the right will be given a rose. There is a wreath and a cross at the front of the church with placeholders for everyone to put their roses in along the sides. Once the rose is placed in either the wreath or the cross, you will fall back in line, then go sit down. Four rows have been reserved for us on the left-hand side of the church behind Kerrie's family. Questions?" When there wasn't any, Bruce continued. "Okay. You'll also be given a piece of paper with a poem written on it. When the pastor gives the signal, we'll all stand up and recite the poem together." Bruce glanced around the small kitchen one more time. When no one said a word, he nodded. "Perfect. Let's all get into line then."

Dan took my hand as we lined up behind Laura and Brad. I accepted the rose Rebecca offered and Dan took the small white piece of paper from Bruce with the handwritten poem on it.

We climbed back up the narrow stairwell that also led to the front lobby of the church. The line stopped, waiting for a cue for us to carry on through two large oak doors into the church. I noticed there wasn't one sound coming from behind those closed doors. No music, no voices—the entire church was deadly quiet, too quiet. It felt odd. My hands began to sweat, and I fought the urge to let go of Dan's hand, to wipe my damp palm on my pants. Instead, I forced myself to focus on the thin stem of the rose clutched in my other hand, in a death grip. When the doors opened, the line started to move and finally Dan and I crossed over the threshold. We walked down the aisle, which led to a large staging area in the front of the church. On the left side stood a podium, where the pastor stood watching our procession make our way towards the front of the church. High on the wall was a large wooden cross with Jesus nailed to it, surrounded by stained glass windows. The pews on either side of the aisle were packed solid with people. I could feel the eyes of everyone on us. Dan and I took small steps together, stopping for a second in between, waiting for whoever was in front of us to place their rose in either the wreath or the cross. It felt like it was taking forever, so instead of meeting the curious gazes of the people we passed by, I stared down at my feet, while waiting for Dan's hand to gently pull me forward. Then it hit me so hard that I gritted my teeth, my mouth forming a straight line.

Kerrie would never walk down the aisle at her *own* wedding. Kerrie would never get married or have a family of her own one day. I swallowed this revelation, that had been launched from my heart and targeted my eyes, making me bit down on my bottom lip. *Not here, not now,* I told myself, holding back tears.

Dan cleared his throat and tugged at my hand. I snapped back to attention. We were next. I purposely watched closely as Laura carefully placed the long stem of her rose in the large flowery cross. The wreath was already full of red roses. A picture of Kerrie, blown-up to poster size, was sitting on an easel right beside a white marble urn. It was her most recent school portrait, her smile lighting up her entire face. *My god, she looks so young.*

Dan let go of my hand. I stepped away from him and in front of the cross, covered in white carnations. With a shaky hand, I tried to stick the stem of the rose into one of the green plastic holders along the side, only to hold back a groan. Unbelievably, I had gripped the rose so tightly that I bent the stem, nearly snapping it in half. When I let go, it almost toppled to the floor. I quickly snatched the flower back, folded the stem in half, and shoved the bent end into the placeholder. When I was sure it would stay put, I stepped back beside Dan, who took my elbow to follow Laura and Brad to our seats. I slid my butt across the wooden bench to sit right up against Brad.

Dan sat on the other side of me. I bowed my head, in time to see Dan run the palms of both his hands on his dress pants before taking my hand again and squeezing it.

The pastor, who was wearing a white robe with a matching white sash around his neck, started the service by welcoming everyone and expressing his deepest and sincere condolences to the Brown family and all of Kerrie's friends. He then spoke about the Lord's unwavering love and mercy and how, with the gift of prayer, God had the power to forgive and to help us heal. I sat up straight, pressing my lower back against the wooden bench, and listened politely. When the pastor read from the Bible, he recited scripture, words strung together that brought me no comfort and no clear answers as to why a good and merciful God would allow Kerrie to die the way she did, without mercy. God had, obviously, been asleep at the wheel the night Kerrie was murdered. I was also unmoved by the pastor's unreasonable religious explanation of Kerrie's untimely death being a part of God's grand plan, that she was in God's kingdom now, which he followed with empty promises that healing could be found through the power of prayer and our almighty God. Listening to him, I realized he didn't know Kerrie at all. I wondered if he had even met her.

I closed my eyes to block out the pastor's hollow words about a girl he never knew to remember her. *Remember Kerrie*, I told myself, taking a deep breath. I saw her face, not the posed school portrait put on display at the front of the church—the real Kerrie—the smiling, laughing, and talking Kerrie. But that was all I saw. I tried to conjure up one bad word she ever said or a sour face she ever made. I couldn't. Kerrie had been a normal teenage girl, living a normal teenage girl's life. Normal. The word struck and stuck, as I realized that Kerrie would never have the chance to become anything but normal. Forever fifteen years old, frozen in time, robbed of the years required to grow old to become something other than normal. Would Kerrie, being a normal teenage girl, be enough to always remember her by? I opened my eyes and turned my head to study all the sullen and sad faces of the people Kerrie had, at one point in her short life, touched.

Did I really know her? No, sadly, I did not. Kerrie and I had shared moments in time where we had breathed the same air, spoken the same teenage giddy girl language, and found common ground within our imperfect families—her mother going blind and my mother leaving town. We liked the same movies, the same music and shared the same friends, but honestly, I did not really know Kerrie. And now, because of God's grand plan, I never would.

I turned to face forward and focused on the back of the heads of the people who *did* know Kerrie. Mr. and Mrs. Brown sat up straight and stiff, with Kerrie's older brothers on either side of them. I hoped, with my entire heart, that the pastor's words that echoed off the high cathedral ceiling would, at least, bring Kerrie's family some comfort.

When one of the two people on this earth who knew Kerrie the best stood up in the front row, she took one small step forward and then stopped. Both her parents jumped up from their seats to position themselves on either side of her, holding her steady as they climbed the two wide steps together. Once behind the protection of the wooden podium, Natalie put down the papers she clutched in one shaky hand to adjust the microphone so it pointed at her face. When she started to speak, I leaned forward in my seat. Her voice stumbled, and her words were muffled. I held my breath as her mom and dad stepped forward to stand on either side of her. Mona placed one hand on her daughter's back. Natalie closed her eyes and bowed her head. The microphone captured the sound of her taking a deep shaky breath in. When she raised her head to face the crowded church, she offered a weak smile. After clearing her throat, she began to read from the crumpled papers in front of her. Her voice becoming a bit louder with each word she spoke and stronger with each sentence she read.

As I watched her, I found myself in awe of her. I knew right then and there that Natalie Zane was the bravest teenage girl I would ever meet. I was moved by the courage it took for her to stand up in front of all these people, to tell stories of her, Rebecca, and Kerrie growing up and going to Eastwood Elementary together. Before her family moved to Spoonbill Crescent, all three of them for a time lived just down the street from one another. Natalie explained how on weekends they would take turns sleeping over at each other's houses and that it had happened so often that they didn't even ask permission from their parents anymore. Natalie told how her dad was a bush pilot, and Kerrie would tag along on many of their family trips to their base camp, to help with their fish packing plant, and to just hang out exploring the northern forest.

With each memory Natalie shared, my heart ached for her. As she spoke about her childhood best friend, her words vibrated with love and how Kerrie's death had not just destroyed the Brown family, but her family as well—Kerrie's second family. Their lives would never be the same again. When Natalie was finished, she wiped the silent tears that slide down her cheeks during the entire eulogy while she clenched the papers in one fist.

It took all my willpower not to jump up to clap and cheer for her.

When it was time for the reading of the poem, it was as if we had rehearsed it a hundred times over. When the pastor nodded at us with outstretched hands, we all stood up at once and, on cue, recited the poem perfectly, together.

> *You left a beautiful memory*
> *And sorrow to behold*
> *And to those who loved you dearly*
> *Your memory will never grow old*
> *Wherever life may take us*
> *Whatever we may do*
> *The memories of the years we shared*
> *Will keep us close to you*

With a final blessing to Kerrie's family and friends, followed by the Lord's prayer, the funeral was over. We stood up and watched as the Brown family left first before we followed behind, leaving the same way we had come in, one row at a time, only at a faster pace. We made our way back down those narrow stairs to the basement dining room. Plates filled with triangle-cut sandwiches along with bowls of pickles and cheese were placed in the middle of each table by the church volunteers who were now busy in the small kitchen.

"Do you want coffee?" Dan asked.

We were standing off to the side, beside an empty table near the stairs.

"Sure." I pulled out a chair to sit down.

"That was goddamn brutal," Chris said, falling into a chair beside me.

I nodded, just as Laura and Brad sat down across from us.

"Natalie did an amazing job," I scanned the tables, trying to see if I could find her. I wanted to tell her myself.

Chris, Brad, and Laura nodded in agreement.

"What are we doing after this?" Laura asked.

Brad shrugged, his tie long gone. "I don't know." He shifted in his seat. "Depends on how long we have to sit here."

Laura slapped his arm. "We at least have to go and pay our respects to Kerrie's parents." She scolded him.

The Brown family were sitting at a table in front of the kitchen, being served by the volunteers as people lined up off to one side, waiting their turn to offer their condolences. Mr. Brown wore a light brown suit and stood behind the table, leaning over it to shake hands while Mrs. Brown sat in the chair beside him. She wore a white dress splattered with blue flowers, her short wavy brownish grey hair framing her pale features. With a blank expression, she stared straight ahead at the people crowding into dining room. A woman I did not recognize stood behind her, then touched her gently on the shoulder before leaning down to whisper in her ear. Mrs. Brown tilted her face upward, and responded with a weak smile on her thin lips—her blindness, more apparent than ever.

I turned my attention back to Chris and Brad, who had already started in on the plate of sandwiches. Food was the last thing on my mind.

"Here you go." Dan placed a Styrofoam cup of black steaming coffee in front of me.

"Thanks." I reached for the cream and sugar in a plastic container in the middle of the table beside a vase of fake flowers.

"Can we hang out at your place after this or are your parents getting sick of us?" Brad chewed with his mouth open.

"Yeah, my parents said it would be okay, but tomorrow is going to be a different story." Dan leaned over to grab the last sandwich.

"Oh?" I asked.

He swallowed. "My mom wants me back in school. No more skipping classes. She's right. It's time to go back."

It felt like forever since we had been in school.

"Yeah, my parents too." Chris reached over to snap up the last pickle before Brad could get it.

I took a sip of my coffee, tuning out of the conversation, feeling exhausted. I could only imagine what the Brown family and Natalie must be feeling.

Dan leaned over to whisper in my ear. "Hey, do you want to get out of here?"

"Shouldn't we go pay our respects to her parents?"

"It'll be a long wait." Dan nodded towards the long line of people waiting their turn.

"Okay." I downed my coffee before pushing my chair back to stand up.

"Meet up with you guys at my place later." Dan stood up.

Laura and Brad both nodded. Chris was already gone.

After finding our coats jammed in with the others in the coat closet, we ran through the bitter cold wind which tried its best to blow us over as we wove our way across the icy parking lot. Once we were in the car, Dan started the engine and rubbed his bare hands together, giving the car time to warm up. The first dump of snow hadn't happened yet. The freezing arctic air that had slapped both our cheeks rosy was a sharp reminder that it was only a matter of time. We sat impatiently, waiting for the warm air to blow through the vents.

"Hey, come over here," Dan ordered.

I moved over to sit right next to him and let him kiss me hard on the lips, grateful it was just the two of us.

When he pulled away, I peered into his blue eyes. "How are you?" I asked breathlessly. His kiss left my lips tingling and my head swirling.

He smiled and raised one eyebrow. "Okay. And you?"

"Exhausted, and it's not even noon yet." I sighed.

"I know, me too." He kissed the tip of my nose.

I rested my head on his shoulder. "Every day there's something else that reminds me what it means for Kerrie to be gone. Like things that happen that Kerrie will never get the chance to do."

"Like what?"

"Like when we were walking down the aisle in the church, it dawned on me that Kerrie will never get married. She will never be a wife. She will never be a mother."

"I know," Dan whispered.

We sat, not saying a word, as the warm air finally started to blow through the vents.

"Hey," Dan said, breaking the comfortable silence between us.

"Hm?" I tilted my head up.

"If you were ever taken like Kerrie, promise me you will do everything you can to get away. Like making yourself throw up or shitting your pants. . ."

"Oh my God!" I said, horrified, pulling away from him, wrinkling my nose in disgust.

"What? I'm being serious." He held up his hands as if I was about to slap him. He wasn't wrong. "I heard somewhere that if you gross them out in some way, they're more likely to leave you alone and possibly let you go."

"That's not only gross, but weird." I groaned. How did the subject change so drastically?

"I know, but IF it were to happen to you. . ."

"It won't and I will," I interrupted him.

"I'm only saying—"

I firmly placed my gloved hand over his mouth. "I promise." I stared into his dreamy blue eyes. "I will make myself puke my guts out or force myself to shit my pants if I am ever abducted. Okay?" I couldn't believe I was promising this to the very first serious boyfriend I ever had.

Dan nodded.

I could feel his smile beneath my glove. "Now, can we change the subject, please? It's kind of killing the mood."

He nodded again.

I took my hand away from his mouth and kissed him before he could say anything else.

The back door of the car whipped open with help from the wind, letting in a whoosh of cold air. Chris, Jade, and Victor crawled into the backseat.

"I'm starting to get a complex with you guys ditching me every chance you get," Chris declared, slamming the door shut once they were all squished together.

"We didn't know you needed a ride," I said, reluctantly pulling away from Dan.

"What are you two lovebirds up to?" Jade teased.

"Can we go for fries and gravy at Chicken Chef? Those sandwiches aren't cutting it," Chris asked.

"I guess so." The disappointment in Dan's voice was apparent as he turned away from me to put his seatbelt on.

I moved back over to the passenger side.

"So, Chicken Chef then?" Dan asked, squinting into the rearview mirror.

"Yes!" I answered loudly, snapping on my seatbelt, "AND Jade is buying!"

"What?!" my sister screeched from the backseat.

"Yes, my dear sweet sister, you *are* buying! Because you owe me twenty bucks for my favourite blue blazer with the shoulder pads." I replied.

CHAPTER 6
WHO THE FUCK IS PAUL STANLEY?

When my alarm clock screamed beside my head Thursday morning, I literally jumped out of bed, almost falling flat on my face. I realized, much too late, that my legs had somehow gotten tangled up in my bed sheets. With my badly choreographed leap into a new day, I was desperate to burst the suffocating bubble of grief that I had been living in for nearly a week. Selfishly, I wanted life to return to some semblance of normal. That feeling, and the heavy load of catch-up homework, were the main reasons that fuelled my desire to get back to school.

As I put my jacket on in the foyer, the sound of car horns honking in the distance drew me back into the living room. I stood in front of the bay window and watched curiously as a convey of cars turned onto Notigi Bay. Dan's car was in the lead, followed by Bruce's Daytona and Buddy's boat, all honking their horns as Dan pulled into my driveway. The other two cars pulled alongside the curb in front of my house.

"What the hell are they doing?" Dad came up beside me drying his hands on a tea towel.

"I have no idea." I pulled my hair out from the collar of my jacket. "Hurry up Jade! Dan's here!" I picked up my bookbag and heading out the door.

"Tell them to stop honking those bloody horns before the neighbours complain!" Dad yelled after me.

I stood on the porch to loop my arm through my book bag strap and hoisted it over my shoulder as Dan stuck his head out the driver's side window.

"They arrested the guy who killed Kerrie!" Dan hit the car horn again.

Bruce and Buddy did the same.

I could now see Tammy and Chris were sitting in the back seat of Dan's car.

Holy shit, I thought, as I flew off the deck, my boots barely grazing each step.

"Who!? When!?" I jumped into the front seat and slammed the door shut. I dropped my bookbag on the floor and turned sideways so I could face all of them, ignoring my seatbelt.

"They arrested Paul Stanley!" Dan was smiling from ear to ear.

"Who the fuck is Paul Stanley?" I scrunched up my face trying to put a face to the name but came up blank. I had never heard of him before.

"He's twenty-two and lives out at the dump," Chris said.

"He lives out at the dump?" A mental picture of a hobo living among piles of garbage materialized in my head.

"His parents do," Dan corrected Chris. "His parents manage the city dump. Paul lives out there with them."

The Thompson city dump was six kilometres south of the city, past the Quarter Mile. When we were little, my dad would take us out for ice cream. He would then drive the short distance south of town to the city's landfill, hoping to catch a glimpse of wild black bears. It was a local attraction and a cheap form of entertainment that rarely disappointed. We would shriek with excitement, with our sticky hands, banging on the car windows, trying to grab the bears' attention while they gorged themselves on the heaps of garbage. I don't ever remember seeing a house out there.

"Dad's freaking out!" my sister announced, climbing into the back seat.

Tammy moved over to sit in the middle, making room for her.

"Quit honking your horn before he has a heart attack," Jade said.

"They arrested Paul Stanley!" Tammy squealed in Jade's face, clapping her hands together. "They caught the guy who killed Kerrie!"

Jade opened her mouth, then closed it, shaking her head. "Never heard of him." She leaned forward, peering past Tammy at Chris. "Have you?"

"Nope," Chris said.

"How did Kerrie know him?" I asked.

"We're not sure." Dan put the car in reverse. "But we're all heading to my place to figure it out. Chris knows the guy who saw Paul coming out of the stables that night. The cops have an *actual* eyewitness, Kat. Someone who saw Paul Stanley leaving the stable road the night Kerrie was murdered."

"What guy?" Jade and I asked together.

"All in due time, ladies. All in due time." Chris cracked his window open an inch and lit a cigarette.

"Why is it always drama and suspense with you, Chris?" my sister asked, annoyed, reaching for her seatbelt.

I gave my sister a sideways glance before turning to put my seatbelt on. Did she not hear the irony in her question? I hated the thought the minute it popped into my head; Jade and Chris were made for each other.

"So, we're not going to school?" I didn't try to hide the disappointment in my voice, the bubble of grief still intact.

"Not yet." Dan backed out of my driveway.

Once settled into our usual spots back in Dan's basement, we listened as Chris told us how David Samson had witnessed Paul Stanley coming out of the stable road on the night Kerrie was murdered.

"How do *you* know David?" Bruce asked.

"I got to know him through the radio station, but also from school. He's in grade eleven and from the Eastwood area. He knew Kerrie from seeing her around the neighbourhood and at the high school. He's big into heavy metal music, and I'm talking a true-blue head banger." Chris paused. Once he had everyone's undivided attention, he continued. "David would come by the radio station to drop off his heavy metal records to play because the radio station doesn't stock them, like Black Sabbath or Metallica. He hangs out with a couple of dudes that are heavy into smoking weed, but I'm pretty sure he doesn't partake. He's a decent enough guy, pretty articulate actually, and quite interesting to talk to. He works part time at the Hillcrest gas station."

Because Chris worked at the radio station, he was somewhat of a local celebrity. It was an occupational hazard, or an occupational opportunity, depending on how you saw it. If people didn't know Chris personally, they certainly knew of him, just by tuning into the CHTM radio station three to four nights a week.

I knew of David, having seen him and his weed-smoking buddies hanging out in the forum at school. Chris was dead on with his description of him. David's appearance screamed head banger, with his acid wash baggy jeans, and loose-fitting, green and black lumber jacket, which he always wore, that hung past his hips. He was a short, husky guy, with poker straight, thin blond hair that fell past his shoulders. His hair was the perfect length to flip back and forth while playing his air guitar to the heavy metal song blasting through his Walkman headphones. Which I had seen him do on more than one occasion, while sitting across from him in the forum.

David reached out to Chris, knowing he was a close friend of Kerrie's, to tell him about what he had told the police the night Kerrie went missing.

He and a few of his buddies were out cruising that night. David was celebrating his parents being out of town that weekend. It was the first time he had no parental supervision for a few days, and was, as he had put it, his time to shine with having full access to the family's red Ford truck that weekend. That night, he had stopped for coffee once or twice at Chicken Chef. At some point in the evening, he had gotten pulled over by the RCMP to perform his first sobriety test by blowing into a breathalyzer, which he passed. Sometime around midnight, David and his buddy, Louie Longhorn, drove out to the cemetery trying to avoid his other buddies who were also driving around. They were all playing car tag. The cemetery was another well-known cruising destination when the city streets became too mundane. It was north of the city, past the Burntwood bridge along the Mystery Lake highway and, as luck would have it, the road to access the graveyard was right across the highway from the stable road.

After navigating the dark, narrow road that wound around the various headstones of Thompson's past residents, David approached the stop sign on the Mystery Lake highway. His headlights were off as he scanned the highway for his friends, with no traffic coming from either direction. He then noticed the outline of two vehicles stopped at the stop sign across the highway, coming out of the stable road. He could only make out the shape of a car, and behind it, a van. Both vehicles had their headlights off as well.

After consulting with Louie, they agreed that the vehicles weren't their buddies. So, David flicked the red Ford truck's headlights back on and the other vehicles did the same. David knew they had the right of way, so he waited, only they didn't go. After a few minutes and muttering a few swear words under his breath, David slammed on the gas pedal and squealed onto the highway to drive back to the city.

"What kind of car was it?" Buddy asked.

"David confessed that he's not a *car guy*. You know, a guy who can see a car and know the year, make, and model, so he wasn't sure. He said it was a big boat of a car, like a muscle car, and he was pretty sure it was green," Chris said.

I glanced over at Buddy. From the look on his face, he was piecing together the reason behind all the questions from the RCMP about his own *boat* of a car.

"There was also a van?" Bruce asked.

Chris nodded. "Yeah, he thinks the van was white, but he wasn't sure because it pulled back and disappeared. The car, however, followed close behind him. Here's where it gets weird." Chris paused for a moment. "Instead of the car just following David back to town, it pulls out and passes him." Chris takes another long drag from his cigarette and looks around the room. "But when the car passes him, it passes him on the shoulder instead of on the road, spitting up rocks. That's when David got a good look at the driver."

"Did David know Paul before?" Buddy asked.

"He said no." Chris shook his head, flicking his cigarette in the large glass ashtray on the coffee table.

"Then how did he know who he was?" Bruce asked.

"When David heard that Kerrie's body was found out near the stables, he called the RCMP to tell them what he had seen that night. The first time he called, all he could tell them was that he had seen two vehicles coming out of the stable road that night, giving them the descriptions of both. It wasn't until he pulled up to get gas and cash a personal cheque—that's when David recognized not just the car, but Paul as being the guy he saw coming out of the stable road that night. He cashed the third-party check, even though he wasn't supposed to, and called the RCMP again to tell them he now *knew* the name of the guy who was driving the car he had seen that night."

"So, they arrested Paul because David saw him coming out of the stable road?" Tammy asked.

"No. And don't quote me on this, but it was after they searched Paul's car and saw a red blood stain on the floor in the backseat." Chris butted out his half-smoked cigarette. "*That's* when they arrested him."

The thought of Kerrie's blood found in Paul Stanley's car sent an icy chill through me. What were the chances that the same guy David had seen leaving the stable road the night of the murder would show up to where he worked a couple of days later to cash a personal cheque?

"Why would he pass David on the shoulder?" Rebecca asked, frowning. "You just kill someone and then you draw attention to yourself by passing on the shoulder, instead of on the road? It doesn't make any sense."

"Maybe he thought if he passed David on the shoulder of the road, he wouldn't be able to get a good look at him?" Bruce suggested.

"Maybe he was drawing attention to himself, to take the attention off the van?" Dan offered.

"Why pass him at all?" Rebecca asked, still not convinced. "Why wouldn't he just hang back and disappear out of sight like the van did?"

"I still don't see the connection between Kerrie and Paul. Paul's what? Twenty-two years old and hasn't been in high school for years," Dan asked, "How would Paul ever meet or know Kerrie?"

"Maybe he had seen her around town or at the TB playing pool? Maybe. . ." Bruce began before he was rudely interrupted.

"*Maybe* Paul was just cruising around town that night and saw her. *Maybe* he tried to pick her up or offer her a ride, and she refused to go with him. *Maybe* he dragged her kicking and screaming into his car? *Maybe* he was searching for a girl to rape and murder that night, and she just happened to be there. OR *maybe* Kerrie was *just* in the wrong place at the wrong fucking time!" Brad's sudden outburst took us all by surprise.

The room went deadly quiet as everyone turned to stare at him.

Bruce went to open his mouth, but when he saw Brad's red face, he shut it.

"Brad!" Laura finally spoke up, breaking the awkward silence in the room.

"What?!" he yelled back at her, then shook his head and lowered his voice. "I don't understand why everyone is so damn stuck on the theory that Kerrie *had* to know whoever did this to her?" His eyes darted around the room. "Honestly? Who do any of *you* know that could do what was done to her? I don't know about you guys, but if I find out that I *actually* know the fucker or fuckers who did this to Kerrie, I'm going to re-evaluate every goddamn friend I have, starting with you *fuckers*." Brad's voice cracked. He bowed his head and covered his face with both hands.

Laura reached over and grabbed his arm, squeezing it hard.

Nobody said anything for a while, as Brad's sharp words sunk in. It seemed more likely that Kerrie was grabbed and taken against her will by someone she *didn't* know. It was hard to believe that someone *we* knew, or who knew *her*, could have murdered her. Brad was right. The thought of actually knowing the person made me sick to my stomach.

"I remember seeing Paul before." Natalie's eerily calm voice cut through the heavy silence in the room.

She was sitting in the leather recliner, the same recliner that Kerrie and she once shared, her knees drawn up to her chest, her arms hugging them. She appeared to be emerging from whatever dark place she had put herself in—showing small signs of the spirited girl she once was. That thick fog of grief was fading or the drugs she had been taking were wearing off.

"Well, I remember the car for sure. Do you remember, Bec?" Natalie asked Rebecca, who was sitting cross-legged on the floor in front of the TV beside Bruce. "It was a big boat of a car. We were waiting for the bus on Princeton Drive last summer. At first, we thought it was Buddy until he circled back around, and we got a good look at the guy?"

Rebecca tilted her head, thinking.

"He drove by us real slow, like he was checking us out," Natalie said.

Rebecca nodded. "I *do* remember that. Didn't you yell at him to take a picture? It would last longer?"

"Sounds right." Natalie smirked. "He was creepy-looking and wore a baseball cap."

Natalie's sudden recollection of having seen Paul Stanley before offered the possibility of a connection between Paul and Kerrie. This proved, at the very least, that Paul knew of Kerrie's existence. A weak connection, but a connection just the same. Add to that, Natalie's off-the-cuff description of Paul being "creepy-looking," which pointed a, albeit crooked, finger of suspicion at him.

The checklist of what a murderer in Thompson, Manitoba might look like formed in my head: white male, possibly a loner—check. Still living with his parents—check. Living at the city dump—check. Creepy-looking—check, check.

"If he had anything to do with Kerrie's murder, then why wouldn't he just dump her body in the mounds of garbage that were in his own backyard?" Tammy asked. "Why leave her in the woods, where she was out in the open, exposed and could be found?"

"I don't know about you, but bringing a body home to Mommy and Daddy's house wouldn't be my first choice. Plus, if her body *was* found at the dump, that would have been harder to explain than where she was found, on the opposite side of the city," Chris said.

"We were lucky Kerrie was found at all," Bruce said flatly.

Another heavy silence fell over the room.

Bruce, of course, was right. With the thick, lush forest surrounding Thompson, it would have been impossible to even hazard a guess to where to start to look for Kerrie if she hadn't been found. Thank God for those ladies who had been out horseback riding that day. If it hadn't been for them, Kerrie could have been lost to us forever. With her being exposed to the elements, not to mention the wild animals that would have tampered with and eventually destroyed all the evidence, including her, it was pure luck that Kerrie was discovered at all.

"If they release him, I say we deal with him ourselves." Geno's voice was cold and deadly. He was standing behind the couch with his thick arms folded across his chest.

"Oh, that makes perfect sense, Geno," my sister snapped at him, shaking her head. "Let's all go to jail for murder. What a brilliant idea."

Geno shot Jade a dirty look.

"Easy, big guy." Chris wrenched his neck upward to smirk at him. "If there's a beating to be given, we are all well aware that *you* would be the one giving it."

Bruce cleared his throat. "Constable Crostini called me yesterday. He wants to meet with all of us at city hall this Sunday night to talk about starting a streetwise group in town."

"A streetwise group?" Brad scoffed. "Meaning what exactly?"

"I'm not sure," Bruce said, "but I think we should at least hear him out. Maybe we could do something for Kerrie, like setting up a scholarship fund in her name at the high school."

"A scholarship for what?" Tammy asked.

Bruce shrugged. "What was Kerrie's favourite subject?" He turned to Natalie.

"English," Natalie said sadly.

Rebecca nodded in agreement.

"So, it could be a scholarship in Kerrie's name for a student graduating with the highest mark in English," Bruce suggested.

"How much money would we have to raise?" Rebecca asked.

"I'm not sure of that either, but we can figure it out later. What should I tell him?" Bruce looked around the room.

"I guess it couldn't hurt to at least listen to what he has to say," Dan said.

Everyone murmured in agreement.

"Okay, I'll let him know," Bruce said.

Shortly after 10:00, Dan pulled into the parking lot behind the high school next to the smoke doors. A few kids were huddled together, trying to create a wind break under a cloud of smoke. There was still twenty minutes before the next class bell rang.

Without shutting the car off, Dan turned in his seat. "What are you thinking about?"

I shrugged. "I know how it sounds, but I just want things to get back to normal. Whatever normal means now." I sighed. "It just feels like we've all been stuck in this bubble, and it can be suffocating at times."

"Yeah, I hear you." He reached over, taking my hand and entwining his fingers with mine. "It's going to take some time, Kat."

"I know." I squeezed his hand. "I mean, even with us, we just started dating, and it's been a whirlwind of emotion and grief and. . ." I shook my head, embarrassed at how I sounded like a whiny kid.

"Hey, I get it. Believe me, I feel it too," he agreed. "But now that they caught Kerrie's killer, things should start calming down a bit."

"So, you think Paul Stanley did it?" I asked.

"I think the RCMP wouldn't have arrested him if they didn't have the evidence," Dan said.

"I guess so," I said.

But I wasn't totally convinced.

CHAPTER 7
WHAT ARE WE SUPPOSED TO DO NOW?

After school on Friday, I headed straight to my room to toss my backpack stuffed with the entire contents of my locker, along with the list of missed assignments on my bed, before going to grab a snack.

Jade was standing in the middle of the kitchen with two green pieces of paper in each hand. "Busted!" she announced when she saw me.

My heart sunk. I knew exactly what she was holding. RD Parker had a student absentee program in which my sister had been an active participant in the year before, being that she was a year ahead of me in school.

After missing two classes, and if no note from the parents was handed in, a green letter would be mailed that would require a parent's signature. If the student continued to miss classes, a yellow letter would then be issued. Again, the official school letter not only required a signature from the parents, but it also came with a stern warning that further action would be taken if unexplained absences continued. If the student's attendance record still did not improve, a pink letter would be mailed. Pink was bad. Pink was very bad. Pink meant, effective immediately, the student was kicked out of the class and could not return until a meeting was set up between the parents and the principal. During the meeting, the student and parents would both have to sign a written attendance contract promising that no more classes would be missed for the remainder of the semester. After missing almost four days of classes, Jade and I were lucky the letters that came in the mail were only green. It was my first warning, and my sister's one of many.

"Did he leave a note?" I asked. Dad had obviously left the letters on the kitchen table for us to find. There were three separate pieces of paper ripped out from his notebook, listing our assigned chores in his familiar messy handwriting, only this time our names were written in capital letters at the top of each and had thick double lines underneath in blue ink.

"Nope." Jade threw the letters back on the table. "We're going to be grounded *for sure!*"

Dad was just finishing up his afternoon shift rotation on Tuesday, which would be followed by five scheduled days off before starting his midnight shift rotation. This meant that he would be home in the evenings next week, with us being securely under his thumb to carry out any sentence he imposed. *At least we had the weekend.*

I picked up my list, my craving for a peanut butter and jam sandwich long gone, as I read what Dad expected me to do. First, I needed to pull my brother away from the TV to get him started on filling the wood boxes behind the fireplace, and then I had to get supper ready. I sighed, thinking about all I had to get done before Dan came over later. My sister left her list where it was and headed to our bedroom to listen to music.

I'd just finished loading the dishwasher after supper when Dad finally called.

"Well?" he asked in his stern, fatherly voice.

I bit my bottom lip while trying to think of an answer.

"May I ask where you and your sister were when you both were supposed to be in school?"

"We were hanging out in Dan's basement." I confessed and sat down at the kitchen table. There was no point in lying to him.

"Just so I'm clear. You both got up and got ready for school each morning—making me believe that you both *were* going to school, but instead, you and your sister went to Dan's house to just hang out?" he asked incredulously.

"Yeah, I guess," I answered meekly. When he put it that way, it sounded worse than it actually was. I instinctively pulled the phone a safe distance away from my ear and braced myself.

After a moment of silence, I pressed the phone back to my ear. "Dad? You still there?" I secretly hoped the phone line had gotten disconnected somehow.

"Where's your sister now?" he asked, his voice surprisingly calm.

"She's getting Jake ready for bed," I lied.

My sister was supposed to be running Jake a bath, only I could hear the music blaring from our bedroom, and my brother was, as always, in front of the TV. At least Jake had finished all his chores.

"I'm disappointed in both of you, but more with *you*, baby girl. I expect something like this from your sister, but not from you."

I felt the sharp knife of guilt hit its target. Since mom left, somehow, I took on the role of being the "responsible one". The "good one" or the "one" Dad could always count on to make sure that Jake was taken care of and that our chore lists were done. The "one" with the added responsibility of also trying to keep my older sister in line, which was near impossible. Dad believed I was the more mature one; when, to be honest, I was just more in tune with what was going on around me, and I also gave a shit. I wisely picked my battles and chose not to openly defy him all the time and on every subject. Why rock the boat when there was no chance of paddling it forward? What was the point of fighting with him all the time and about everything? I also felt sorry for my dad. All he was trying to do was raise us all by himself, and some days I could see the physical toll it was taking on him. So, to get along, I did my chores, followed curfew, and stayed under the radar whenever possible. It also helped that my sister, who always demanded the spotlight, kept me safely in her shadow. Plus, I just didn't see the point of pissing him off all the time.

"It goes without saying that you both are grounded indefinitely, so don't make any plans to go out this weekend," he said.

"I know." I was relieved, because it was going to take me all weekend to get caught up on my homework.

"Tell your sister that there is no point in arguing with me about it. I will be home in the evenings next week to make sure you both stay put."

"Okay." I stood up, getting ready to hang up.

"Did either of you know this Paul Stanley that was arrested for Kerrie's murder?" he asked.

"No." I replied, surprised by his question.

"Me neither. I checked to see if he worked here at the mine. He doesn't."

"Oh." It was all I could think to say. It made sense that my dad would wonder if he worked for INCO because most of the male population in the city was employed there. It was likely going to be the career path for some of the guys I hung out with.

"Do you know who I thought it was?" Dad asked.

"Who?" I was a bit surprised that my father had his own opinion about who could have killed Kerrie.

"Remember that guy who was phoning you last summer trying to ask you out on a date?" Dad asked.

"Dalton Johnson." I whispered the name and sat back down.

How could I have forgotten about him? Dalton Johnson was in his early twenties and reeked of what I referred to as the Ick Factor. The Ick Factor was when you meet someone, usually a guy, who would, for some unexplained reason, make the hairs on the back of your neck and your arms stand straight up. This sixth sense warning you with an icky feeling that something was "off" or "just not right" about that person.

I didn't know Dalton Johnson even existed until, out of the blue, he called me one night last summer to ask me out on a date. He had apparently looked up my phone number in the phone book after seeing me play pool at the TB. When I figured out who he was—a black man who was tall and thin with short curly black hair and a face littered with acne scars—I was put off right away, the needle to the Ick Factor buried deep, simply because of the age gap between us. He admitted, yeah, he was in his twenties, so what? When I told him how old I was, it didn't seem to bother him at all. In the past, I had been mistaken, once or twice, with looking older than my fourteen years, but not by that much. I politely declined his offer for me to meet up with him somewhere away from my house, so as not to alert my parents. Only Dalton didn't give up that easily, calling me a couple more times, insisting he would show me a good time if I would *just* give him a chance.

After the third phone call, and unable to convince him I really was not interested in going out with him, I went to my dad for help. I explained to my over-protective father that some older guy had been calling me, wanting to take me out on a date. I left out a few details, of course, of Dalton seeing me playing pool at the TB in my skin-tight jeans. My dad told me to tell him yes the next time Dalton called and to agree to meet him wherever he suggested. And that if my dad happened to be home, the next time he called, he wanted to listen in on the phone conversation.

A couple of nights later, just as I was finishing the supper dishes, Dalton called again. I took the call in the kitchen and my dad quietly picked up the phone in the living room, covering the mouthpiece with his hand to listen. Doing exactly what my dad had told me to do, I pretended to cave and agreed to meet Dalton later that night in the Safeway parking, which was only three blocks from my house.

Shortly before 8:00 p.m., Dad got up from his favourite spot on the couch to go and meet the twenty-something man who was hell-bent on dating his fourteen-year-old daughter. When Dad came through the front door a half an hour later with a bucket of Napoleon ice cream, all he said was, "Dalton won't be bothering you anymore."

That was the end of it.

"Honestly, I had completely forgotten about Dalton," I said.

"I know, me too, until I heard about Paul Stanley's arrest. Dalton is roughly around the same age as Paul Stanley, which just made me wonder who else might have been involved with Kerrie's murder."

I wondered about that myself.

Dalton's name never came up when we had tossed around potential suspects while sitting around in Dan's basement. Why had he slipped my mind? He was in his twenties, had been out of school for a couple years, and wouldn't have shown up at Dan's party, which was full of high school kids. Or would he have? Dalton didn't have any direct contact with Kerrie or anyone else in our group, at least none that I knew of. But then again, neither did Paul Stanley. The only difference was that Dalton sometimes hung out at the TB, and if he had noticed me, then maybe he had noticed Kerrie, too.

"Okay, baby girl, I gotta go. Don't forget to tell your sister to stay put." Dad's voice broke the train of my racing thoughts.

"I will," I promised, knowing it was another lie.

When Dan came over later that night, I told him about Dalton Johnson.

"I can't believe I forgot all about him until my dad mentioned him." I was sitting on the couch with my legs stretched across his lap. My brother was watching TV on the floor, and my sister was talking on the phone in our bedroom. "Do you think the cops even know about him?"

"I don't know." Dan shrugged. "I'm sure they're looking at everyone."

"But what if no one has even mentioned Dalton to them?"

"They arrested Paul. I'm thinking they had enough evidence to do that. If Dalton was there or had anything to do with it, it will eventually come out." Dan assured me.

"Do you know what Dalton drives?" I was not ready to give up on the subject. "What about the van? Do we know of anyone that drives a white van?"

"Mark Bernard drives a white van." My sister plopped down in the chair across from us, letting her long legs dangle over the arm of the chair. "Someone wrote 'murderer' in the dirt on a window of his van today at school. I saw it when I went out for a smoke."

"That's crazy!" I was shocked. Obviously, word had gotten around school about the vehicles David had seen coming out of the stables that night.

Mark was a tall, lanky guy with short, thick brown hair and a pasty complexion. Like David Samson, I only knew him to see him, either sitting in the forum or in passing in the hallways at school. He did drive a white van. I wondered if the RCMP had talked to him.

"Everyone in this stupid town is going crazy! It's so unfair!" My sister threw up her hands. "Did you tell your boyfriend about Dad's latest lock down sentence?"

Dan turned his attention back to me and raised one eyebrow.

I scowled at Jade. "Both of us are grounded, indefinitely." I confessed. How was I supposed to date a senior in high school when I was grounded or on lock down all the time? How long would it be until Dan finally got fed up and broke up with me? "The green letters came this week, and because Dad's on afternoons, we couldn't intercept them."

Our mail was delivered to the Gingerbread House around noon each weekday. Jade had taught me the schedule of our neighbourhood postal delivery service last year, when she knew an absence letter was coming, and she couldn't make it home for lunch in time to intercept it. She would ask me to get it, which I did for her many times, always doing what was expected of any loyal sister. Then I would watch in utter amazement as she forged my dad's signature perfectly. If I had to guess, I had intercepted at least seven green letters out of her eight scheduled classes last year. If only my sister used her powers for good instead of evil.

"Do you think Derf might ease up for one night to let you guys go to the meeting at city hall on Sunday?" Dan asked.

"I don't know." I shrugged. "But I'll ask." After getting caught skipping classes, I was pretty sure I knew what Dad's answer was going to be. Plus, the meeting was on a school night—the odds were against us.

"If *I* ask, it will be no for sure. If Katrina asks, then we might have a fighting chance," my sister said with a pout on her lips.

"Whatever." I shot her a look that clearly meant "shut up".

"You know it's true! Dad *always* listens to *you*," Jade whined and pointed a thumb at Dan. "Look who's a year younger than me and is allowed to have a boyfriend."

"For the record, Dad thinks Dan is a friend of both of ours, and not my boyfriend. So, he's not knowingly letting me date him." Jade had a knack for making herself look like the victim in any situation. "Maybe your boyfriend should have the balls to introduce himself to Dad, like Dan did."

"Yeah, right!" my sister said, horrified. "Dad LOVES to intimidate anyone we bring home, girl or boy. And if I thought he wouldn't put poor Vic through the third degree, I would let him, but what's the point? Dad would say no anyway."

"Fine. Then shut up about it," I snapped at her. "Enough with the *poor Jade* routine. I'm sick of hearing it."

"Hey guys, no need to fight over me," Dan said nervously.

"Oh my God, *you* wish!" my sister snapped at him, before turning back to me. "You have to admit that our dear old dad has literally gone bat-shit crazy since Kerrie's murder. And now that they arrested the guy who killed her, he needs to calm down. All I'm saying is that if he heard it from his favourite daughter, then he would listen, because he never listens to me."

Dan shifted in his seat, either because he felt uncomfortable or because of the weight of my legs across his lap.

I lifted my legs off him and swung around to glare at her. "Maybe he listens to me because I don't fight with him all the time. Maybe he doesn't listen to *you* because *you* don't cut him any slack or HEY, I KNOW!" I slapped my forehead as if the idea had just come to me. "Maybe if you did your chores like you're supposed to, didn't skip school, sneak out, or didn't break curfew all the fucking time, then just maybe he would listen to *you* and cut *you* some slack!"

"If you guys can't make it to the meeting," Dan chimed in, "I can fill you both in on what happens."

Jade stood up and put both hands on her hips and glared down at me.

I glared right back.

"Whatever. I'm going to Victor's house," she said and stomped out of the living room.

"When Dad calls to check in, I'm not covering for you!" I yelled after her.

"He just called. He's working a double!" she yelled back before slamming our bedroom door.

I smiled at Dan. "Are you thinking what I'm thinking?"

He shook his head and smiled back. "Ah, what are you thinking?"

"Let's blow this popsicle stand!" I jumped up, took his hand and pulled him up off the couch, and then dragged him to the foyer to grab our jackets. We bolted out the front door before my sister could.

After we bought slushes from Southwood, a popular convenience/ice cream store, Dan and I cruised around, talking.

"Just out of curiosity, do you think your dad is over-reacting or, as your sister put it, going bat shit crazy?" Dan asked.

"No, I don't," I shook my head. "He's just scared, that's all. But if he was going bat-shit crazy, it's only because he fathered the spawn of Satan."

Dan chuckled. "Sometimes I have to remind myself who is older—you or Jade."

"I have to remind myself every day of my life!"

"My parents are talking about selling the house," he said, changing the subject.

"Really?"

"Yeah, they've been talking about it for a while now, but with everything that's going on, I think it's gonna happen sooner than later," Dan said. "They've been looking at houses in the Riverside area."

"Makes sense." I shook my slushy, trying to get the block of ice in my cup back into liquid form.

Dan's dad was a successful businessman, who owned a thriving construction company in town. When Dan's mom wasn't working in the family business, she spent the rest of her time doting on Dan and his two younger sisters. When I was around Mrs. Safflower, I couldn't stop myself from studying her from out of the corner of my eye. I always felt nervous and awkward around her. Not because she was pretty with her short reddish blond hair cut into a stylish bob or because she had Dan's blue eyes or because she was always kind to me, talking to me in that soothing motherly voice. No, she was the mom I wished my own mother could be. For that reason alone, I was jealous of Dan.

When Dan started to complain about how both his parents were putting pressure on him to get his applications in for university next fall, I quietly listened. He was applying to a couple of schools down south, and was excited about leaving Thompson next fall, but not happy about leaving me. The thought of him moving away made me sad too, but again, Dan was lucky. University was never going to be in my future, especially with my mediocre grades. It also didn't help that I was aware of what the first and second mortgage payments were on the Gingerbread House each month. Money was a constant struggle at our house, especially after Mom left, and

Dad having to pay her out a small fortune in the divorce. I made the mistake one time of asking Dad for some money for fries and gravy. He dug in his pocket for loose change and held it out to me. When I began to dig through the loose change to pick out the quarters and loonies, he told me that both mortgage payments were due the next day. I dropped the coins back into his large hand and went to my room to get my babysitting money that I secretly stashed under my mattress in a sock, so that my sister couldn't find it.

"School really sucks," Dan said as he turned onto my street to drop me off. It was almost eleven o'clock.

I wondered if my dad had phoned, and if Jade had stuck up for me, even though I took off, leaving her to watch Jake.

"You know what sucks more?" I asked.

"What?"

"Poverty," I said.

He laughed. "Good point." He pulled into my driveway.

I peered through the windshield and my heart sped up. "Something's wrong," I said. Every light in the house was on, which wasn't right at this time of night. I jumped out of the car and raced towards the house and bolted up the porch steps.

When I burst through the front door and into the living room, I found my little brother crying loudly sitting on the couch with big Geno sitting right beside him. Geno's enormous arm was draped over my brother's small shoulders. He was trying to console Jake but wasn't doing a very good job of it. My sister stood in front of the fireplace, her face paler than usual, and her eyes were red and puffy, like she had been crying too.

"What the hell happened?" I looked at my sister, then at Geno, who I saw had no shirt on, which was very disturbing. I was shocked at the amount of thick, black, curly hair that covered his upper chest. His chest hair was pitch black against the whiteness of his bare skin.

"This big idiot thought it would be funny to scare the shit out of us," my sister spat at Geno.

"What?" I asked, totally confused.

Dan hurried through the front door and stood beside me.

"I was only joking around." Geno shrugged. "How was I supposed to know this little guy was still up?" He spoke to Dan instead of me.

"What the hell are you talking about?" I asked, losing patience, I went to sit on the other side of Jake, who leaned into me. I wrapped my arms around my little brother and hugged him hard. The volume of his crying lowered to muffled whimpers as he shoved his face in my armpit. I glared at Geno and waited.

Geno pulled a mask out from behind his back and held it up. It was one of those scary Halloween rubber masks you pulled over your entire head. It was completely bald, with holes cut out for the eyes with a crooked nose, and an opening for a mouth with fanged teeth. Fake blood dripped from each corner of the mouth opening and down its pointy chin.

"I took off my shirt, put on the mask and burst through the door, but no one was around," Geno explained sheepishly, "I thought you and your sister were in your room. I honestly forgot all about Jake. So, I locked the door and started to bang on it, waiting for one of you to come and answer it."

"Oh my god!" My eyes widened because I knew exactly what had happened next.

By mistake Jade or I would sometimes lock the glass door that separated the living room from the foyer before going to bed, which would force my dad to bang on it to wake one of us up to let him in, usually in the middle of the night. The key to the door was lost a long time ago. Jake must have heard the banging first and thought it was Dad locked out again. Half asleep he went to let what he thought was our father in, only instead, Jake had unwittingly let the big, scary, and very hairy Geno into our house—wearing that god-awful mask—which made Jake freak out and scream like he was being murdered. If it had been me, I would have screamed my bloody head off, too.

"Where were you?" I asked my sister.

"In our bedroom, talking on the phone with Vic when I heard Jake scream. I tried to get to him, but our bedroom door got stuck somehow and I couldn't get the door open. When I finally got it open, Geno was standing in the hallway, still wearing that stupid mask." She wrapped her arms around herself and squeezed.

"She punched me in the face, twice, before I realized I was still wearing it," Geno added, as if punching him in the face was the worst thing that happened that night.

"Good," I said through clenched teeth.

"Can I sleep with you tonight?" Jake asked my armpit.

"You sure can, bud," I said, hugging him close while shooting death daggers at Geno.

"What the hell were you thinking?" Dan glared down at him, shaking his head.

"We were just fooling around, that's all." Geno stood up.

Dan crossed his arms in front of his chest and locked eyes with Geno.

"I told him it was a bad idea." Bruce interrupted the tension building in the living room, coming out of the kitchen with a glass of water in one hand.

Jake sat up, took the glass from him with shaky hands, and gulped the water down.

"You'll be okay, little buddy," Geno said, leaning down to pat my little brother roughly on his small shoulder.

I slapped Geno's hand away. This time, instead of saying it under my breath, I said it right to his face. "You're an asshole."

***

As per usual, Jade was completely wrong about the power I had over our father.

Sunday morning at breakfast, I tried to convince him to let Jade and me go to the meeting that night at city hall, but Dad wouldn't budge.

"You girls need to learn that what I say goes." He placed a platter of his famous French toast in the middle of the table before taking his seat at the head of the table. "Besides that, you both need to focus on getting your homework done. I spoke with the principal and assured him that both of you will be caught up with your assignments by Monday." He reached over and stabbed a piece of bread with his fork.

"I promise we'll be caught up before the meeting." I meant it. "Constable Crostini just wants to meet with us for a couple of hours to discuss the idea of us starting a streetwise group in town. The meeting is at City Hall." I added this last bit of information, thinking it might impress him.

It didn't. "Your first priority is school, not starting a streetwise group." He cut up the thickly sliced bread now smothered in butter and syrup. "Elbows off the table, Jake."

Jake dropped his elbows off the table.

Dad was strict about using proper table manners: elbows off the table, chew with your mouth closed, no talking with your mouth full, and always, always having to politely ask before being given permission to leave the table. The main rule, of course, being we were to eat whatever was put in front of us because of all the "goddamn kids starving on a continent on the other side of the world."

"This is such bullshit." My sister pushed the bacon around her plate with the tip of her fork.

"What was that?" My father stared across the table at her, his fork in mid-air.

Switch flipped. I sighed. *Here we go again.*

"What?" she asked, the expression on her face fell somewhere between innocent and guilty.

He turned his fork to point it at her, a piece of bread dripping with syrup dangling at the end of it. "Don't look at me in that *tone* of voice, young lady!" He barked, using one of his go-to phrases when we glared at him or rolled our eyes.

We were all too familiar with Dad's one-liners or catch phrases that he would hurl at us, to confuse us or make us stop arguing with him, derailing what we were going to say. How can a look have a tone of voice? Of course, this is what he intended by deflecting or distracting us. It was just another one of his parenting tricks that he had up his sleeve when it came to winning any argument against us.

He was the master of deflection. For example, when we were smaller and our arguments would escalate, he would declare a wrestling match in the middle of our living room to redirect our anger and turn it into a physical play-fighting match. In the living room, he pushed furniture back and out of the way, as we all piled on top of him—trying to take him down. Even though the odds were always against him, three to one, he always managed to flip one of us over to pin one of us down. He would then secure our arms under his knees while balancing on top of us, careful not to crush us under his weight. Then with both fists circling the air just above our face, he would give us a choice in our surrender: "sudden death" or "hospital", the names he had given each fist—which would leave us all out of breath and laughing.

"Dad!" I raised my voice just a little, trying to get the conversation back on track. Why did my sister feel the need to get him all riled up? Once his IT was unleashed, there was no reasoning with him. "All I'm saying is that Constable Crostini wants to talk to us first about possibly starting a streetwise group. And we were also thinking about getting a scholarship fund set up in Kerrie's name at the high school. Dan can drive us."

Dad turned, narrowing his eyes at me and lowered his fork. "And ALL I am saying is NO. End of discussion." He then shoved the bread into his mouth.

Jade shifted in her seat while my brother glanced around the table at all of us.

"May I please be excused?" my sister asked politely. She had barely touched her breakfast.

"Fine," Dad said, choosing to ignore the food she was about to waste along with his standard question: Do you know how many kids in Africa are starving right now? Followed by, we should all be bloody grateful for the food he put in front of us. Instead, he just kept on eating.

Jade got up and scraped her plate loudly into the garbage before dropping it in the kitchen sink with a loud clang.

I watched her in disbelief. If she kept this up, we would never leave this house again.

"AND if either of you skip another class, I will be notified *by phone*. No more letters in the mail," Dad barked between bites.

"Yes, sir!" My sister stood up straight then raised her right hand to her forehead in an officer's salute. "Anything else, sir?!"

Jake covered his mouth with one hand to stifle a giggle.

I shook my head. My sister just didn't know when to quit.

Dad's mouth formed into that thin straight line, his face turning a bright shade of pink. "Yeah, one more thing," he said through gritted teeth. "Remember, young lady. I brought *you* into this world and I can sure as hell take *you* out."

"Understood!" Jade shouted back at him before she stormed out of the kitchen.

"Until things calm down around this bloody town, I want all my kids home under this roof where I know where they are and are safe. Is that too much to goddamn ask?" Dad muttered under his breath as he stabbed another piece of bread off his plate.

"Didn't the police catch the guy who killed Sister's friend?" Jake asked.

The expression on my father's face changed as his head shot up to look across the table at my brother. "I sure as hell hope so, bud," he replied, his voice no longer angry.

***

As promised, Dan phoned late Sunday night once he got home from the meeting at city hall. I'd been in my bedroom waiting for his call and managed to snap the phone up in the middle of the first ring. Dad was in the living room with the TV blaring, watching his favourite show, *Matlock*.

Dad had done the "Fake Out" earlier that afternoon, pretending to leave for work and then coming home with a pizza for supper instead. This successfully squashed our plans to go to the meeting anyway, without his permission. While he was setting the table, I pretended to go wash my hands but instead slipped into my bedroom to quickly dial Dan's number to tell him not to come get us. Dad had taken the night off from work and was home to make sure we didn't go.

"Hello," I whispered into the phone, as I strained with my other ear to listen for any sudden changes in the TV's volume.

"Well, we all agreed to form a streetwise group," Dan said, without saying hello first.

"You did?" I flopped back down on my bed, my head sinking into my pillow, stretching the phone cord to its limit.

"*We* did," he corrected me.

"Okay."

"The mayor was even there, Katrina!" Dan sounded as if some celebrity had shown up. "He said if we started the streetwise group, he would give us full access to the city council chambers to hold our meetings. He's hoping, with us agreeing to do this, that something positive will come out of what happened to Kerrie. A streetwise group could do just that, by bringing awareness to all the kids in the city."

"And how exactly do we do that?" I asked, the volume of the TV still loud and blaring from the living room. "How can we bring any more awareness to the city? Kerrie's murder is all anyone is talking about."

"That's the whole point. It wouldn't just be about Kerrie's murder. It would be about educating kids in town about street safety and raising awareness of the possible dangers. Oh, and the scholarship fund for Kerrie was also brought up," he added. "They offered to help us set it up. All we have to do is raise the money." The more he talked, the more excited he sounded.

I listened, playing with the phone cord.

"It's a good idea, Kat," Dan finally said.

"It sounds like a good idea," I agreed. "I'm just not sure if I'll ever be allowed to join, thanks to Jade. We'll be lucky if we're allowed to leave the house before Christmas." I glanced over at my sister, who, without looking up from the book she was reading, promptly gave me the middle finger.

"Our first official meeting is a week from today. I'm thinking Derf should be calmed down by then. We're going to elect a president, and treasurer and all that. Oh, your name came up for the secretary position."

"Me?" I asked, surprised.

"Yeah, why not?"

Why not? I wondered what we were getting ourselves into.

After hanging up, I crawled under my covers and turned over onto my side, pulling my pillow over my head to block out my sister's reading lamp.

When she finally turned it off, I rolled onto my back and stared blindly at the ceiling, wide awake.

After a while, I heard the TV in the front room shut off, followed by Dad's heavy footsteps as he went to the kitchen to put whatever dishes he had collected during the evening in the sink.

I turned onto my side and closed my eyes when he opened our bedroom door. He stood in our doorway, something he had done a thousand times before, to check on his daughters before turning in for the night. I could feel the burden of being a single father radiating off him. Without having to open my eyes, I could see his large dark silhouette. Once he was satisfied that we were both sleeping, safe and sound in our beds, he shut the door.

I moved onto my stomach and shoved my face into my pillow, willing myself to go to sleep, trying to ignore the grating sound of my sister snoring a few feet away.

The streetwise group seemed like a good idea, but I had no clue what it meant. We were all going to patrol the city streets of Thompson with flashlights, wearing high-visibility vests, to stop any more murders from happening in town? Obviously not, but in all honesty, with Kerrie's killer now behind bars, what were we supposed to do now? Just move on with our lives, without Kerrie?

The police arresting Paul Stanley didn't change a goddamn thing. I flipped over onto my back, blinking into focus the patterns of the moonlight dancing across my bedroom ceiling. Whatever we chose to do next—start a streetwise group, raise money for a scholarship fund for Kerrie, or even apply for university next year—absolutely nothing would change the fact that Kerrie would still be gone. Forever.

CHAPTER 8
YOUTH FOR A BETTER TOMORROW

From the moment the reality of what happened to Kerrie sunk in, a small part of me felt like I didn't belong to her inner circle of friends. I had known Kerrie for just a few short months before she was killed. Yes, I was devastated by her death and mourned her deeply, yet there was a small part of me that questioned if I had earned my place in this tight-knit group of kids united by grief and sorrow. At times, I didn't think so.

That feeling of doubt shifted with the streetwise group. I oddly felt a renewed sense of purpose, which brought with it the thought that just maybe something good could come from her murder. I also had this unsettling need to do something, anything, to pay tribute to a young girl taken from the world so senselessly, regardless of how short-lived our friendship had been.

Over time, Kerrie's friends seemed to come to terms with her death in their own way. The streetwise group would give us a collective goal to move forward together with a positive purpose. It would also distract us from the gaping hole Kerrie had left behind. With her accused killer behind bars, what else could we do?

After a week on lock down in the Gingerbread House, Jade and I were both granted early release because of good behaviour, just in time for the first official streetwise meeting in November.

At city hall, the council chamber was a formal meeting room used by the elected officials to oversee the day-to-day running of Thompson, Manitoba. After stepping through the heavy double oak doors and across the threshold, I was immediately impressed by the room's décor. There were large windows that lined one side of the room, taking up the top half of the entire wall, framing the city's blinking night lights. In the far left-hand corner, behind an elevated desk, sat a black leather high-back chair with the Manitoba flag on one side and the Canadian flag on the other. The empty prominent seat behind an oak desk was reserved for the highest position in city office. Two long oak tables extended from either side of the mayor's spot, each with leather seats and microphones poking out from the tables. On the opposite side of the room, six rows of a dozen chairs allowed citizens to watch the proceedings.

Jim and Ann Brown took up two seats in the front row while teens piled in beside and behind them. Constable Crostini, in full uniform, stood off to the side, leaning up against the window's ledge, his tall, lean frame set against the backdrop of the city lights. He was the lead investigator on Kerrie's case and was only there, unofficially, to assist us with the initial setup of the group.

The first order of business was to elect leadership positions. Being the natural leader of our group, Bruce began the meeting by taking his position in front of the gallery with the empty elected officials' seats behind him. Not surprisingly, Bruce was the first to be voted in as our president by a show of hands. This was followed by Dan, who was voted in as the public relations officer. Chris Jones accepted the advertising seat. Next up was Tom Waters, who nodded his acceptance of the treasurer's role. Tom was a short, chubby guy with a close to the scalp tight cap of curly black hair and a pale complexion, who always wore thick, black-rimmed glasses. Tom was too quiet, which made him almost invisible in our group. He was an honour roll student who could easily pass as a middle-aged accountant. I accepted the nomination for secretary, and once voted in, I began taking notes, having brought a notebook and pen with me. Both Dan and Jade had convinced me that because I was always writing, it only made sense that I record the minutes of our meetings.

Once we were settled into our elected seats, the next order of new business was to vote on a name that would best represent the group and what our goals were going to be. "Think of your common purpose," Constable Crostini said from the sidelines. After a half an hour of discussion, we decided our mission would be twofold: first, to bring safety awareness to the city's youth; and second, to raise money for a scholarship fund in Kerrie's name to honour her memory. Once recorded in the minutes, various names for the streetwise group were shouted out and openly debated.

With each name, a motion was put forward, which was followed by either Bruce, Dan, Tom, Chris, or me seconding that motion. Only then could an official vote take place with the members, in favour or not in favour. The name that raised the most hands was Youth for a Better Tomorrow (YFBT).

For the scholarship fund, we voted to raise ten thousand dollars. The money would be used to purchase a bond at a local bank and the annual accumulated interest would be awarded to the high school graduate who achieved the highest mark in English. Our first official target date for Youth for a Better Tomorrow was to raise the money in time to award the first Kerrie Ann Brown Memorial Scholarship in June to a student in the graduating class of 1987.

The question of how we were going to bring awareness to the youth in Thompson caused a murmur of confused voices among us. Constable Crostini stepped forward to suggest we could start by sharing our story with other youth in the community. This would help to bring awareness to other kids like us and prevent what happened to Kerrie from happening to anyone else. We would need to focus on the dangers of walking home alone and ensure there was clear communication between friends and family regarding our whereabouts. He offered to work with our newly elected president on how this could be set up in the future.

When the meeting began to wind down, Mr. Brown stood up from his chair. A handful of teens were already getting up to leave, but when they saw him, they quickly sat back down.

"If I may, I just wanted to take this opportunity to say..." He stopped and bowed his head.

The room fell into a respectful silence.

After a moment, he cleared his throat, lifted his head, and his glossy brown eyes swept across the room, blinking back tears. "What *we* just wanted to say is that we've been deeply moved by the outpouring of love and support we've received since losing Kerrie. We truly had no idea how many friends Kerrie had, how many lives she touched, or how much she meant to so many people." His voice wavered, but he quickly regained his composure.

"Ann and I are so deeply touched by all of *you kids* and what you're doing here tonight—not just keeping Kerrie's memory alive with the scholarship fund but also starting this streetwise group. It means so much to us that what happened to Kerrie never happens to another family in this city."

Mr. Brown's gaze fixed briefly on Constable Crostini before he gruffly concluded by pledging the first five hundred dollars to kick-start the scholarship fund.

When he sat down, Mrs. Brown raised her hand blindly, which he reached up to grasp with his own. He lowered their hands onto his lap while wiping the tears from the corners of his eyes with his other hand.

Mr. Brown's heartfelt speech and generosity made everyone stand up to clap, cheer, and whistle, adjourning the first official meeting of Youth for a Better Tomorrow.

***

Over the next few weeks, YFBT put together a Christmas bake sale. Everyone baked up a storm on Friday night, only to get up early on Saturday morning to go to the mall and set up tables.

After the bake sale, a 50/50 draw was organized. A fundraiser where whatever monies collected by selling raffle tickets would be shared evenly with the winner and YFBT. The fundraiser made us all split up and spread out throughout the city once again, only this time to sell tickets. We sold every one of them long before the draw date, which was a few days before Christmas.

YFBT was also given permission to place donation jars at local businesses around town, which added to the growing bank account and increased Youth for a Better Tomorrow's exposure within the community. Chris set up an interview with Bruce on the radio, so he could introduce the newly formed youth group to the residents of the city. Articles were also written about us in *The Thompson Citizen*.

With YFBT's introduction to the city, a whole new set of teenage rules—just for us—came into play. Before, we had lived in anonymity, under a fluffy cloud of ignorant teenage bliss. As the youth group's popularity grew, we soon realized that we were now out in the open and exposed, with a bright shiny spotlight pointed at each of us—from our peers, the high school faculty, the community, the RCMP, and local businesses. To gain and maintain our good standing in the public eye, we had to prove that we were, in fact, the responsible young adults we had inadvertently claimed ourselves to be. Everything we did could and would affect Youth for a Better Tomorrow's success. We not only had to talk the talk, but we had to walk the walk.

Instead of partying or cruising the city streets, we met at Chicken Chief for coffee or in Dan's basement to organize future fundraising events. Instead of playing endless card games of asshole in the forum at the school, we put our heads together to compile a list of new business items for YFBT's agenda for the next bi-weekly meeting. We did all of this while balancing our schoolwork, home lives, and part-time jobs.

With New Year's fast approaching—a holiday which would typically be celebrated by attending the annual social at the Legend Hall or a pre-organized house party—instead, YFBT organized a babysitting night at the local YMCA. The entire main floor of the building was offered to us by the local organization, which could accommodate up to thirty kids. We began advertising the New Year's Eve Babysitting Bash, offering a night of games and fun activities to help bring in the new year with thirty excited children. This allowed the parents to enjoy their own celebrations and ring in the new year, child-free. The night was a tremendous success and raised over a thousand dollars.

Our own parties were now few and far between. When we did manage to pull ourselves together with a couple cases of beer to split between us, it was done so quietly. The freedom to be goofy teenagers, to party hard, or to play car tag on the city streets was over. Even the smoke-filled air in Dan's basement smelled different—stuffy, even—with the music turned down low and our singing silenced. The immature stories we used to share with each other about our daily teenage antics weren't as funny anymore. The happy-go-lucky existence we had taken for granted was long gone. No matter how hard we tried to recapture that party atmosphere or carefree teenage feeling, Kerrie's glaring absence always hung heavy in the air, especially when we were all together. How could we just carry on without her? We couldn't.

A prime example was when we helped Mona organize a surprise party for Natalie's fifteenth birthday in February. It wasn't a milestone birthday, but it would be the first birthday Natalie would celebrate without her best friend by her side. The party was also an attempt to keep Natalie from falling into that heavy, thick fog of grief and guilt. In preparation, we filled Natalie's basement with pink streamers and balloons. Mere minutes after we had all screamed "SURPRISE!" and jumped out from our respective hiding places, the doorbell rang from upstairs, interrupting the celebration.

A strong feeling of déjà vu filled the air as the music was turned off, followed by everyone shushing each other loudly. We then heard Mona's angry voice travelling down the stairs after she had opened the door to find two RCMP officers in full uniform asking to speak to her daughter.

After Natalie had slowly climbed back up the stairs, we sat in stunned silence, listening as one officer serve her with a subpoena that requested Natalie Ann Zane to appear as a witness for the Crown in the upcoming preliminary hearing of Paul Stanley, who was charged with the first-degree murder of Kerrie Ann Brown. Each one of us wore the same mortified expression as we shook our heads in utter disbelief at the poor timing of it all.

Mona's sharp response was quick and brutal. She called the police out with a few swear words for their blatant insensitivity, albeit without reason. How were the officers to know it was Natalie's birthday? Mona dismissed them by thanking them for ruining her daughter's surprise birthday party. Unwittingly, Mona had informed the officers that other potential witnesses may also be present. In response to Mona's harshness, one officer yelled down the basement stairs, calling the names of other kids on their subpoena list.

When the officers finally left, half the kids in the basement sat dumbfounded, holding subpoenas of their own. None of us were in the mood to party after that, as Kerrie's glaring absence from her childhood best friend's birthday celebration was more apparent than ever.

***

After the holiday season, Dan, Bruce, and I were asked to speak at the six elementary schools in the city. As promised, Constable Crostini had reached out to the Mystery Lake school board, suggesting an invitation be given to the newly formed streetwise group. By telling our story in assemblies at each school, we would have an opportunity to share our story and bring safety awareness to other the youth within the community.

I had never spoken in public before and was a bit nervous at first. But once I was standing in front of the rows of grade six to grade eight students, who sat restlessly on the gymnasium floor, I relaxed for some unexplained reason. I watched as the teachers positioned themselves at the end of each row to ensure attention was maintained throughout the assembly. Calmly, I scanned the young faces that stared up at me while waiting for the cue from the school's principal to start. I couldn't help but think that it wasn't that long ago that Kerrie had been one of them.

To ease into our new roles of public speaking, Dan, Bruce, and I took turns talking. Each of us recited the script we had scribbled out on napkins while sitting in Chicken Chef for hours, drinking countless cups of coffee. The speech, written in bullet points, recounted the events of the night of October 16th, with the message being that what happened to Kerrie could happen to anyone. We spoke about the gap in communication that had caused the confusion among her friends and family about Kerrie's whereabouts that night, and the reason no one knew she was missing until long after she was gone. At each elementary school, we ended our speech with the most important lesson that we had learned from losing Kerrie: *"Watch out for each other, keep tabs on each other, and make sure the people who care about you the most—your close friends and family—know where you are at all times."*

As we worked our way through the elementary schools, my unexplained calmness was soon replaced with a feeling of empowerment, as I understood the importance of what we were doing. By speaking to kids just like us, we were bringing awareness to the city's youth. In doing so, we were working towards Youth for a Better Tomorrow's primary goal: doing everything within our power to prevent what happened to Kerrie from ever happening to anyone else.

When we stood in front of the student body at the last elementary school, Eastwood School—Kerrie's old school—I had just begun to pick up the pace with my part of the script when, out of the corner of my eye, I caught a glimpse of a curly blonde-haired girl sitting cross-legged in the front row. The resemblance to Kerrie was uncanny, which made me fumble my words and stop mid-sentence as I tried to catch my breath. Without missing a beat, Dan stepped forward and picked up where I had left off, giving me time to compose myself. I closed my eyes and took a deep breath, praying that wherever Kerrie was, she was proud of what we were trying to do in her memory.

***

Youth for a Better Tomorrow was always being approached by local businesses, who would offer up suggestions on different fundraising ideas that would align with their business practises to help us raise money. The most intriguing offer came from the provincial government's Forestry Department, known in Manitoba as Manfor.

A representative from Manfor had contacted Bruce to see if YFBT would be interested in venturing out into the northern forest to harvest purple pinecones for their tree refurbishment program. Once the pinecones were picked and gathered into large canvas bags, Manfor would pay us a dollar amount per bushel. The idea intrigued the group. And, after discussing it at length during a meeting in January, the votes were cast, and everyone sat in favour of at least giving it a try that upcoming Sunday.

First thing Sunday morning, nine of us, dressed in our heavy snow suits and with three cars packed with coolers, met at the Shamrock Restaurant on the south side of the city. We had a hot breakfast before heading down the snow-packed highway to spend the day in the bush picking purple pinecones.

The turnoff to Joey Lake was forty kilometres south of the city. When Dan slowed down to take the turn onto the one-lane, poorly maintained road, the car almost slid off the highway. He slowed down to a crawl to stay a safe distance behind Bruce's Daytona. Ron McKenzie, driving his parents' car, followed Dan's lead, also keeping a safe distance behind us. After fifteen minutes, we stopped alongside a huge clearing in the bush, where pine trees had been cut down and scattered about.

I let out a sigh of relief when Dan put the car in park and leaned forward, squinting through the windshield, outlined in frost. Straight ahead and right in front of us was an impressively large steep hill. The narrow road without much warning shot upward in a straight incline, making it impossible to see any further up the road. The road appeared to carry on up into the blue sky, making it hard to tell where the road ended, and the sky began.

Bruce got out of his car and shuffled toward us in his winter boots, pulling the straps of his ski pants back over his shoulders. He leaned down by Dan's cracked-open window. "I'm thinking that we set up an area in the middle of the clearing and start a fire. The girls can sit around it to pick the pinecones while the guys drag the trees over to them," Bruce said.

"Sounds good." Dan nodded while pulling on his toque.

"Be careful getting out on your side, Kat. The ditch is deceiving. It's pretty steep." He smiled over at me.

"Got it," I said, pulling on my winter boots.

It didn't take long to set up a pinecone-picking production area in the middle of the clearing. With our coolers filled with drinks and snacks nearby and a fire raging in the middle, it was pretty warm and cozy. Despite the temperature dipping to minus twenty degrees Celsius, there wasn't a wisp of wind under the clear sunny blue sky. The guys eventually ditched their heavy winter jackets, becoming overheated from the exertion of dragging the cut-down pine trees to the girls, who picked them clean.

We picked and picked and picked purple pinecones until our fingers ached.

"Explain to me again why they have to be purple?" Rebecca asked, holding up a perfectly shaped pinecone in the deepest shade of purple that she had plucked from a branch that lay across her lap.

"For the seeds inside. They bake them in an oven to open the pinecone up, shake out the seeds on a conveyor belt, then plant them to grow baby trees," Bruce explained, sitting on a cooler beside her, eating a charred hot dog.

"They replant them? Out here?" Rebecca asked, turning her head to survey the surrounding clearing.

"Once they become babies, yeah. Manfor is environmentally obligated to replant whatever they harvest from the forest. So, they grow them in a greenhouse first, and once they become seedlings, then they replant them out here." Bruce popped the remaining overcooked hot dog in his mouth.

"I always thought the forest was self-sufficient," Rebecca said.

"It's supposed to be, but because nature isn't prepared for Manfor to come in and hack down so many of its trees at an alarming rate, they are required to replace what they take from the forest." Bruce winked at her before standing up and putting his skidoo mitts back on.

After a productive day out in the fresh air, we gathered up our things an hour before sunset. Everyone was in good spirits and happy with the day's proceeds. By doing a quick calculation in his head, Bruce figured we had made close to five hundred dollars from the almost-three bushels of purple pinecones we had picked and gathered into huge canvas bags provided by Manfor.

Our day out in the northern wilderness not only gave us a chance to hang out and be ourselves—away from the public eye—it also allowed us to raise money for Kerrie. As Geno and Bruce kicked snow over the fire, everyone eagerly agreed to sign on for a few more weekends, not knowing how that one unanimous decision would put all our lives in danger.

CHAPTER 9
UNCHARTERED TERRITORY

At the end of February, Kerrie's friends found themselves once again in unchartered territory: the preliminary hearing of Paul Stanley, charged with the first-degree murder of Kerrie Ann Brown.

I had never stepped foot into a courtroom before and, unlike Thompson's city council chambers, I was immediately unimpressed. The room was rectangular and bore no resemblance to the elaborate courtrooms, accented in oak wood, that I had seen on various TV shows or movies. The room's plain décor consisted of four beige bare walls with no windows, and it was stuffed in the basement of the provincial building, just off Mystery Lake Road and within the same vicinity as city hall.

We entered the room through two heavy steel doors. The highest seat in the court was front and centre on the opposite wall, with a high back leather chair behind an elevated desk that faced the gallery. The gallery had eight rows of a dozen chairs split in two by a narrow aisle. To the right, next to the judge's seat, was a square box outlined in fake wood I assumed was the witness stand because of its position beside the judge, which also faced the gallery. On the left side of the room and up against the wall was another matching wood box, a meter in height, with an empty chair confined in it, waiting for the accused. The area right in front of the judge was separated by two long wooden tables, like the ones in biology class, and on opposite sides—one for the defence attorney and the other for the Crown prosecution. Opposite the accused, on the room's right side, another long table was pushed up against the wall, covered with various items in plastic bags.

Shortly after we took our seats, Kerrie's friends filling up four rows behind the Crown prosecution's table, a hush fell over the courtroom. Paul Stanley, handcuffed, entered from a hidden door on the right side of the courtroom, led by a uniformed officer.

He wore a loose-fitting grey business suit, his short brown hair combed back and away from his face, exposing his pale and deeply weathered features. He had dark circles under both his eyes. His face held no expression as he sat up straight in the wooden box, purposely staring straight ahead at the bare wall above the evidence table.

From where I was sitting, I could only see the right-side of his face. He did not look towards the gallery or even at his lawyer, who sat a few feet away from him. Paul Stanley's lawyer, with his thick salt and pepper hair, kept his head down, not acknowledging his client had even entered the courtroom, as he continued to write something down on a legal notepad.

Like everyone else, it was all I could do but stare at Paul. I narrowed my eyes to study his expressionless profile, searching for any physical sign of guilt or innocence. I knew the idea was stupid, and after a while, I gave up. There was nothing in his stoic, expressionless face that was familiar to me. I had never seen him before. And there was not one distinguishing mark or glaring physical trait about the man accused of killing Kerrie that hinted towards his guilt or innocence. To me, he looked like a regular joe, minus the handcuffs, a guy who was waiting for a job interview instead of a judicial hearing that would determine if there was sufficient evidence to support proceeding to a murder trial.

My gaze fell on the back of Mr. Brown's head, who sat in the front row behind the Crown prosecutor. Kerrie's dad's head was turned sharply, staring, or rather glaring, at the man accused of murdering his daughter. The pure, utter hatred coming off him made me shift uncomfortably in my seat. Dan reached over and took my hand and squeezed it.

With the words "All Rise!" the judge entered the courtroom wearing a black flowing robe, just like all the other judges I had seen on TV. Everyone in the courtroom stood up. After calling the proceedings to order, and with everyone sitting back down, the housekeeping items were discussed in detail and at length, as the week's schedule was reviewed, and the order of witness testimonies was determined.

It was during this three-way drawn-out discussion that the lean defence attorney, who stood over six feet tall, announced that Mr. Stanley would not be taking the stand in his own defence during the hearing. A low murmur rippled through the gallery as I glanced over at Paul Stanley, curious, wondering why. Why wouldn't he want to testify, at the very least, so he could tell his side of the story? Why wouldn't he want to take the stand to declare his innocence if, in fact, he didn't do it? If it was me, I would want to stand up in front of the whole world and scream as loud as I could that I didn't do it, especially if I was innocent.

While the judge and lawyers went back and forth on the week's schedule, I noticed a middle-aged woman with a perfectly round face and short brown hair sitting in front and off to the side of the judge facing the gallery. She held something that appeared to be a funnel with a long handle in one hand. The minute someone spoke, she pushed the funnel against her mouth and nose, then her jaw would move up and down. It took me a minute to understand what she was doing and what her position was in the court proceedings. She was the court reporter, and she was repeating every word being said into that funnel thingy. I had never seen anything like it. In any of the courtroom dramas that I had watched on TV, there was always a smartly dressed woman with long red fingernails madly typing while recording the official court proceedings, and sometimes, she would be asked to read back what was said.

The first witness called by the Crown was one of the women who had come across Kerrie's body early Saturday afternoon. She and a friend had been out riding their horses with a small group of people all morning. But instead of heading back to the stables with the others, the two women continued on their own, steering their horses towards the hydro line. As she retold her story, she stopped periodically to drag a ball of Kleenex under her nose. She explained how her horse had started to act strange and had reared up and stopped abruptly to stomp its feet, obviously uneasy about something. That's when she noticed someone lying a few metres away in the bush. She thought at first it was a mannequin, the kind in clothing store windows, that someone must have thrown away. It wasn't uncommon for people to dump garbage out there. However, once she got off her horse and got closer to the life-sized doll, she realized it was, in fact, the body of a young girl.

She testified she was careful not to touch the body much, as she knew that was important, and only placed two fingers on three different spots to check for signs of life, even though she could tell Kerrie wasn't breathing and hadn't been for a while. Kerrie was very cold under her gentle touch. After confirming Kerrie was dead, the witness then noticed how clean Kerrie's clothes were. The woman thought that was very odd, considering where Kerrie was. Kerrie was lying face down on something. She wasn't sure what, a blanket maybe? Her hair was soaked through, and matted down with so much blood that she couldn't say for certain what her actual hair colour was, but it appeared to be red. She could see that she had been beaten quite badly on her head and face, and one of her arms appeared to be broken because of how it was positioned down by her side.

Through a steady stream of tears, the woman confessed that she had felt the need to sit with Kerrie for a few minutes, telling her how so very sorry she was that this had happened to her before going to get help.

The atmosphere was somber when the woman left the courtroom, still crying and visibly shaken. My heart ached for her as I watched her leave.

After the morning break, Natalie Zane was called to the stand.

I bit my bottom lip, as she was sworn in with her right hand lying flat on a Bible held out in front of her. Natalie wore black stirrup pants with a long navy-blue blouse. Her long brown hair fell loosely around her pale features, draped across her shoulders and down her back. I leaned forward in my seat. That cloud of fog had returned and surrounded Natalie. Her eyes appeared hazy and held no expression. When she sat down, she crossed her legs and folded her hands in her lap, then blinked at the Crown prosecutor like she was trying to keep his face in focus.

The prosecutor began by establishing who Natalie Zane was, by asking her to state her full name and address. The Crown prosecutor then added, addressing the court that Natalie was the "last person to see Kerrie Ann Brown alive."

Natalie flinched.

As the prosecutor questioned Natalie, his voice held a steady tone of kindness as he patiently walked her through the day's events of October 16th, 1986, which ended with her, Rebecca and Kerrie attending the party on Trout Ave.

In a shaky voice, Natalie testified about how Kerrie had gotten upset when Chad showed up at the party holding hands with his new girlfriend and how she just wanted to leave. Natalie retold, for the millionth time, how she had forgotten her purse and by the time she had gone to get it and returned to the top of the stairs, Kerrie was gone.

The prosecutor then drew Natalie's attention back to that summer day when she, Rebecca and Kerrie were waiting for the bus on Princeton Drive to go to the mall on a Saturday afternoon.

Natalie testified how this guy kept driving by them "real slow like" as if he was checking them out. She then described what the man driving looked like. She ended her emotionless testimony by pointing a finger with a shaky hand at Paul Stanley.

When the defence lawyer stood up, he started by telling Natalie how truly sorry he was for the loss of her childhood friend, and that he only had a couple of questions for her.

Natalie's shoulders relaxed a little.

"How many times did this car drive past you that day on Princeton Drive?"

"A couple," Natalie said.

"So, two times?"

Natalie nodded.

"I'm sorry, Ms. Zane. The court reporter needs you to respond verbally to my questions for her to record them," he said sharply.

"Yes, twice." Natalie cleared her throat and sat up straight.

"And how long would you say it took each time for this car to pass by?" he asked.

Natalie appeared to think about it for a moment before answering, "I'm not sure."

"Ten seconds, fifteen seconds, a minute?" the defence lawyer offered, with a hint of impatience.

"I'm not sure," Natalie repeated.

"Okay, let's just say one minute each time." Still standing behind the defence table, the defence lawyer paused to refer to his legal notepad on the table. "If the car drove past you two times, with a minute added to each time, this would add up to two minutes total, to identify my client as being the driver of the car, would you agree?" he asked quickly.

Natalie frowned at him before she answered. "Yes."

"And it is your testimony in this courtroom today that it was Paul Stanley that you saw that day driving by you, Kerrie and Rebecca at the bus stop?" he asked abruptly and then looked down again at his notepad again.

"It looked like him," Natalie said.

The defence lawyer's head shot up, narrowing his eyes at her. "Like him?"

Natalie shifted in her seat.

The lawyer moved from out behind the table to stand in front of her, towering over her. "Ms. Zane, when positively identifying someone, especially in a court of law, it does not include the words 'like him.' You must testify with some degree of certainty that you saw it was my client that day, or it was not."

Natalie stared up at him and said nothing.

"I'm going to rephrase the question, Ms. Zane. Are you certain it was Paul Stanley you saw driving by you that day on Princeton Drive?" the defence lawyer asked.

After a moment of deafening silence, Natalie whispered, "No."

"Thank you, Ms. Zane." Paul Stanley's lawyer turned on his heel and went to stand back behind the defence table. "Again, Ms. Zane, I am so sorry for your loss." He sat down.

My heart ached for Natalie as I watched her rise from the witness stand, her eyes now glossed over with tears. I turned to glare at the back of the defence lawyer's head, totally hating him. From that point on, in my head, I referred to him as the Prick.

Rebecca was up next, and when she took the stand and swore to tell the whole truth and nothing but the truth, her eyes were clear, and her cheeks were rosy pink. She sat up straight and answered the same questions that had been asked of Natalie, only in a clear and steady voice.

The Prick stood up and repeated, with the same fake sincerity, how sorry he was for her loss, blah blah blah, before he proceeded to rip apart her testimony as well.

"How many times would you say the car drove by you, Natalie, and Kerrie that day?" he asked.

"A couple times," Rebecca said.

"So that would mean two times, right?"

"Yes, that means two times." Rebecca nodded.

"Or was it four times?" the Prick asked.

Rebecca wrinkled her nose, confused by his question.

"Let me clarify the question I just posed to you. The car drove by you once, then turned around to drive by again. Or did it loop around again and then drive by again? Making it four times the car drove by."

"Uh, I believe it was just two times total," she said.

"So, not four times, but two times?" the Prick confirmed.

"Yes."

"What was the colour of the car?" he asked.

"A light brown colour or a gold colour," Rebecca said.

"Can you be more specific? Was it a light brown or a gold colour?"

"It was more like a tan colour, so a light brown," she said.

"Was it tan, light brown, or gold?" the Prick asked.

Rebecca's mouth opened, then closed, her lips set in a straight line. "A tan colour," she answered stiffly.

"To clarify Ms. Tenor, your testimony under oath today is that the car you witnessed driving by you and your friends twice that day, where the colour of the car started out, in your own words, as a light brown, then turned to gold, then back to light brown, and now your final description of the colour of the car is being a tan colour?" he summarized.

Rebecca's face turned from a pale pink to a bright red. "Yes."

"I have no more questions, your honour." The Prick sat down.

At lunch, in the cafeteria on the main floor of the provincial building, I dropped my tray on the table in front of Dan, who was already sitting down and eating a sandwich. "That defence lawyer is a prick," I said, loud enough for anyone to hear.

Dan's eyes went wide as he stopped chewing and glanced around.

On the far side of the cafeteria sat the defence attorney, with a couple of other people I did not recognize.

"He's just doing his job," Dan said, reaching for his milk carton.

"He can still do his job without being a prick," I said flatly, unwrapping my sandwich.

"If Nat and Rebecca aren't sure, then that needs to be said," Bruce said, putting his tray down and sitting beside me.

"Oh, please tell me more. Oh, mature and wise one," I said sarcastically, shaking my head at him.

Bruce raised both eyebrows and took a deep breath. "All I'm saying is that if Nat and Bec are not sure, then they're not sure, and that's okay, especially if it's the truth."

"And all I'm saying is the prick could have established that without being a complete asshole. Both of them have gone through enough and the last thing they need is for some big city lawyer in a thousand-dollar suit to badger them on the stand and upset them in front of everyone," I snapped at Bruce, purposely ignoring the look Dan gave me. I took a huge bite of my stale ham and cheese sandwich before washing it down with chocolate milk.

When the coroner took the stand after lunch, the temperature in the courtroom dropped well below freezing as he began to testify, in graphic detail, describing Kerrie's injuries that contributed to her cause of death. He would stop to take a sip of water with a steady hand or to refer to his notes, which amplified the deafening silence in the courtroom. If a pin had dropped during these professionally timed pauses, the court reporter could have easily heard it and recorded it.

Kerrie's wounds were consistent with blunt force trauma to her head and face. When further examining her wounds, the size and depth of her injuries indicated the instruments used were of different shapes and sizes and were not consistent with one single weapon. There were pieces of bark and remnants of leaves found deep within her scalp, which supported the finding that the murder weapons used to attack Kerrie were tree branches and logs of various shapes and sizes, taken from the surrounding trees noted at the crime scene. The murder weapons, covered with Kerrie's blood and hair, now preserved in plastic bags, lay on the evidence table.

Paul Stanley's eyes sunk into his expressionless face as he continued to stare straight ahead.

Defensive wounds were found on Kerrie's body that showed she had tried to fight off her attackers. Skin scraped from under her fingernails and markings found on her forearms both proved she had scratched her attackers and raised both of her arms in an attempt to fend off the attack.

Physical evidence collected during the autopsy supported that Kerrie had been sexually assaulted. Semen samples were recovered from her person and her underwear, which showed that she had been redressed after the sexual assault. Other proof to support this was that the clothing she wore was remarkably clean, considering the environment she was found in. One of her running shoes had come off, yet her exposed ankle sock was a bright white, with not a speck of dirt on it. Based on this, it was concluded Kerrie had been sexually assaulted in another location, before being brought out to the woods where she was subsequently beaten to death.

Forensic evidence found at the scene proved that where she was attacked and where she was found were in two different locations at the crime scene. This was determined by the blood splatter pattern on the surrounding trees that were a few yards away from where she was found. The crime scene analysis supported this finding, that she had been moved after the attack by her assailants. The coroner continued, in his professionally controlled voice, by stating that Kerrie was still alive, in all probability unconscious with the severity of her head injuries, when she was placed face down on her jacket and left out in the harsh elements.

There was a sharp gasp, followed by a low moan from someone behind me. I didn't dare turn around, frozen in my seat, scared that if I moved, I was going to throw up. Kerrie was still alive when they left her!? *She was still alive and all by herself, left alone in the dark woods?* I bit down hard on my bottom lip and swallowed the ham and cheese sandwich threatening to come back up. The coroner was far from being finished.

The time of death was determined to be in the late hours of Friday morning based on the body's core temperature and state of rigour when Kerrie was examined, which made the estimated time of the attack between the hours of 11:00 p.m. and 1:00 a.m. Evidence to support this timeline and that Kerrie had, in fact, been alive for several hours after the attack, was determined by the maturing of the bruises that were noted and recorded on her body during the autopsy. The amount of blood that had pooled under the skin's surface showed that the bruises left on her body had fully formed, which could take up to six to eight hours.

The coroner's voice held no emotion with the words he spoke, even with the sudden gasps or quiet sobs coming from the gallery during his entire testimony.

At the end of the long exhausting day, Dan and I sat in the freezing cold car not saying a word while we waited for the warm air to clear off the frosted windshield.

"I'm glad Kerrie is dead," Dan blurted out. His sharp words cut through the bitter cold air between us.

I jerked my head sideways to stare at him. My mouth fell open, utterly shocked by what he had just said.

He turned to look me dead in the eyes. "How could Kerrie have gone through all that and come back to us, normal? How could she have survived something like that and ever be normal again? How could anyone get over something like that?"

I bowed my head, blinking away the tears that had been waiting all afternoon to come. Deep down I knew there was some truth to what Dan said, but being glad that Kerrie was dead, didn't feel right either. "I guess we'll never know," I whispered not knowing what else to say.

That night, under a heavy blanket of darkness and with my sister snoring close by, I lay awake staring up at the ceiling. This time, instead of willing sleep to come, I was desperately fighting it off. I was terrified that the new images of Kerrie's last moments would invade my dreams, turning them into nightmares. I blinked up at the ceiling, feeling my chest grow heavy with each breath, filling my lungs with pure hatred towards whoever had killed Kerrie. Only monsters could be capable of doing what had been done to her, and then to leave her out there, all by herself, still alive and breathing, to die. What kept me tossing then turning into the wee hours of the morning was that if Paul Stanley *was* one of those monsters—he sure as hell didn't look like one.

***

Constable Crostini took the stand the next day, first explaining to the court the police's standard operating procedure for evidence collection, then detailing each piece of evidence that was collected at the crime scene. He would refer to the blown-up photos of the area where Kerrie was found that were put on display in the courtroom, matching the evidence collected to where it was found at the scene. He described in detail the police procedures for handling, collecting and recording each piece of evidence within an investigation such as this one.

During this line of questioning from the Crown, the lead investigator was asked about a single coarse black hair that had been taken from Kerrie's body.

Dan leaned forward in his chair beside me.

The constable cleared his throat, shifted in his seat, and explained that he believed the coarse black hair retrieved had either come from the blanket used to cover her body at the scene or from the body bag used to transport Kerrie to the city morgue. He explained that it was standard procedure to wash body bags before reusing them.

The Crown moved on, asking him to walk through the steps of his investigation, steps that included interviewing various witnesses, which led to the questioning and the ultimate arrest of Paul Stanley.

The constable took his time when describing how David Samson had initially contacted the RCMP regarding seeing two vehicles leaving the stable road on the night Kerrie Ann Brown disappeared. He moved on to recount the second phone call Mr. Samson made when Mr. Stanley showed up at his place of work to cash a cheque, which then put a name to the driver of the car. After taking Mr. Samson's sworn statement, he questioned Mr. Stanley. During the subsequent search of Mr. Stanley's vehicle, a red stain, which appeared to be blood, was discovered on the floor in the backseat. Upon further search of the car, officers recovered two blonde hairs that were proved to be consistent with Kerrie's blonde hair. Conflicting and unreliable witnesses statements taken to account for Mr. Stanley's whereabouts on the evening of October 16th, ultimately led to his arrest for the first-degree murder of Kerrie Ann Brown.

"Based on the evidence collected and the witness statements, I am confident that Paul Stanley is the perpetrator, or one of the perpetrators, involved in the murder of Kerrie Ann Brown," Constable Crostini concluded.

Within the gallery, I sensed a collective sigh of triumph, fuelled by the air of confidence that emanated off Constable Crostini, which matched his authoritative tone throughout his entire testimony. The gallery silently agreed that the RCMP had, in fact, gotten their man.

"In conclusion, Constable Crostini, can you state in this courtroom today that there were no other leads, or witness statements, or other pieces of evidence that would have led you to another viable suspect during your investigation into Kerrie Ann Brown's murder?" the Crown asked.

Constable Crostini sat up straight in his chair. "No, there was nothing presented to me during the investigation that pointed in any other direction. If there had been, I would have followed up on it."

When the Prick stood up, Constable Crostini folded his hands loosely on his lap.

"Constable Crostini, is it correct that you were the head investigator in the murder investigation of Kerrie Ann Brown?"

"I was the lead investigator on Kerrie's case, not the head," he corrected. "RCMP officer Butt was the head of the investigation. Constable Butt was assigned as the general investigator, overseeing the entire unit that investigated Kerrie's case."

The Prick bowed his head and tapped the notepad with one long finger before he continued. "Can you explain to this courtroom what your role would be as the lead investigator?"

"My initial role was to secure the area where the body was discovered. I was the first officer on the scene that afternoon. I was tasked with securing the crime scene and overseeing all the evidence that was collected, ensuring it was recorded properly, then tagged correctly before being placed into evidence," Constable Crostini stated for the second time during his testimony.

"And did you?" the Prick asked, stepping out from behind the table.

"I'm sorry. I don't understand the question," the constable said.

"Let me rephrase. Did you secure the area? Did you ensure there was no contamination at the scene where the victim's body was found?"

The constable sat up and cleared his throat. "You have to understand in terms of size, it was a pretty big crime scene and also extremely challenging since the location was outside city limits in an area that is basically wilderness."

The Prick nodded. "I understand the area that you described in great detail in the courtroom today would be difficult to secure and ensure it wasn't contaminated. But again, I will repeat my question for the third time. Did you, Constable Crostini, secure the crime scene, ensuring there was no contamination from other RCMP officers that were called out to assist you?"

"To the best of my ability, the crime scene was secured," the constable answered.

"So, your fellow officers didn't walk around the area freely, trampling on evidence, or possibly vomited near or at the scene?" the Prick asked.

"I did not witness any such actions by my fellow officers. If I had, I would have stopped it," Constable Crostini said sharply.

The Prick moved on. "Earlier you testified you were tasked within your role as the lead investigator with the collection and tagging of all evidence, correct?"

"That's correct."

The Prick walked back to the table and picked up a file, flipped it opened and returned to stand in front of the witness.

"The coarse black hair that was recovered off the body, you believe came from either the body bag Kerrie was transported in or the blanket she was covered in at the scene, correct?"

"Yes."

"How, may I ask, did you come to *believe* that?" the Prick asked.

"I guess I'll take responsibility for that. The blanket used to cover the body came from the hospital and not from the standard evidence collection kit. It was my mistake. Also, it is standard procedure to wash out the body bags and to reuse them. I believe the black hair recovered from Kerrie most likely came from either the blanket or the recycled body bag."

"Interesting choice of words for a lead investigator, Constable Crostini—most likely," he said. "Within your testimony today, sir, you cannot definitively state that the black hair recovered from the victim's body, in fact, came from the blanket or the body bag—isn't that correct, sir?"

"No, I cannot," Constable Crostini said.

The Prick slammed the file shut, strode back to the table to toss the file on it, then turned back to face the witness. "Let's move on to the other hairs that were submitted into evidence, shall we? The two blonde hairs recovered from inside of my client's car—can you tell this court exactly where those two hairs were found?"

"The backseat," the constable replied.

"Yes, but where exactly in the back seat—on the seat itself, on the door handle, on the floor?" the Prick asked.

"I did not collect the hairs. Our forensic team did," the constable said.

"Would you be surprised to learn that the two blond hairs that were discovered and bagged and tagged into evidence, under your authority, were in fact found under the factory installed carpet in the backseat?" the Prick asked.

"As I stated before, I did not recover the hairs from Mr. Stanley's car," he said flatly.

"Earlier, you testified that it was your role as the lead investigator to oversee all the evidence collected. Would it not be a fair statement that you, sir, should have been aware of where exactly in the backseat the hairs were collected?"

"I did not recover the evidence," the constable repeated.

"You weren't even curious where exactly the hairs were found? You didn't ask the forensic team?"

"The blonde hairs recovered were tagged into evidence as being confined in the backseat of Mr. Stanley's car," the constable said.

"If you had inquired to the exact location of where the hairs were recovered, would you have still issued a warrant for my client's arrest?" the Prick asked.

"Yes, as the hairs proved to be consistent with Kerrie Ann Browns and it wasn't the only evidence that pointed towards your client," the constable said confidently.

"Yes, I am getting to that other evidence, thank you. But first, the blonde hairs that were recovered from under the factory laid carpet that were consistent with the victim's hair were in fact not a definitive match to Kerrie Ann Brown, which in a court of law, such as these preceding, would be deemed as circumstantial evidence, correct?"

"Yes," Constable Crostini reluctantly agreed.

Satisfied with the lead investigator's answer, the Prick moved on to the red stain discovered on the floor in the backseat of his client's car when the RCMP performed the initial search of the vehicle. The defence attorney first pointed out, turning to address the gallery, that his client had agreed to the search of his vehicle willingly and without hesitation and had not requested a warrant, which was within his legal right to do.

Constable Crostini did not respond, as there was no question for him to answer.

The Prick continued. "The red stain that was first noticed by your officers…"

"Which appeared to be a fresh blood stain," Constable Crostini interrupted.

The Prick raised one hand. "Yes, but did your officers notice anything else near that red stain on the floor in the backseat to tip them off as to what the stain could be?"

"I don't recall," the constable said.

"Under your authority and to your knowledge, there was nothing collected and tagged into evidence that was found near that red stain," the Prick asked, impatiently.

"No, nothing that I can recall," the constable clarified.

"Like a small can of V8 juice? The size of can that one would use to pack in, let's say, a lunch bag?" the Prick asked.

"As I have stated, I don't recall any such item being tagged into evidence. The stain on the floor in the backseat of your client's car appeared to be a fresh blood stain."

The defence attorney nodded. "When in fact that red stain when tested and analyzed by a forensic lab—a lab, staffed by professionals trained in the science of forensics—not by hot-headed, narrow-minded RCMP officers, proved to be in fact tomato-based, such as, oh let's just say for arguments' sake V8 juice," the Prick said.

Constable Crostini opened his mouth, closed it, and took a deep breath before answering. "That is correct," he replied.

"Constable Crostini, is it fair to state within this courtroom today and, by your testimony, that you had no other viable leads that perhaps required further investigation into Ms. Brown's murder, besides my client?" the Prick asked.

"That is correct." The constable nodded.

"There were no phone tips regarding the murder taken from the RCMP call centre, not one piece of evidence collected and tagged under your authority, no other RCMP officers indicated to you or Officer Butt, head of this investigation, that would point to any other potential suspects or witnesses during your investigation?" the Prick clarified.

"No," Constable Crostini said firmly.

Paul Stanley's lawyer, in a matter of forty-five minutes, had cast doubt on every piece of physical evidence that could connect his client to Kerrie. The dense dark shadow of doubt hung over the entire courtroom, choking everyone sitting in the gallery into a frustrated silence.

When Constable Crostini was excused from the witness stand, I watched, amazed, and a bit confused, as the lead investigator on Kerrie's murder case walked out of the courtroom still surrounded by that arrogant air of self-confidence and with his head held high. The total sum of his testimony under cross-examination left me no other choice but to have to agree with the Prick, which pissed me off.

The RCMP had no smoking gun, no shocking piece of evidence to prove without a doubt that Paul Stanley had killed Kerrie, or that he even knew her—unless, of course, they had a credible star witness who could put Paul at the stables on the night that Kerrie was murdered.

When David Samson entered the courtroom, the air became electrified with anticipation. Everyone in the gallery turned in their seats to watch the seventeen-year-old saunter down the narrow aisle to take the witness stand.

David cleaned up nicely. His straight sandy blond hair had recently been trimmed and now grazed the tops of his shoulders. He wore new acid wash jeans with a plain blue shirt instead of his usual heavy metal T-shirts that showed off his favourite rock bands like Metallica, ACDC or Black Sabbath. His clean-cut look gave him the appearance of being a respectable young man. When he spoke, I was impressed by how articulate he was. He answered each question in a clear, steady voice with just the right amount of conviction. After only a few minutes of listening to David on the witness stand, I could easily understand why he earned the title "star witness."

The prosecutor took his time guiding David through the night Kerrie went missing, starting with him cruising Thompson's city streets with his friend Louie Longhorn. David spoke directly to the gallery as he described his first experience of being stopped by the police that night and made to perform a sobriety test. He added that it was the one and only test in his entire life he didn't have to study for and passed with flying colours. The fact that he kept the blow piece as a memento sent a murmur of giggles throughout the gallery, and a smirk from the court reporter.

David explained the reason for him and Louie being at that particular stop sign on Cemetery Road around midnight on the night of October 16th. They were in the midst of playing a rather intense vehicular football car tag game with two other cars loaded with his buddies—which David was determined to win. It was also why his headlights were off as he crept up to that stop sign on the Mystery Lake Highway. He then described the vehicles he noticed across the highway, coming out of the stable road, with their headlights off as well. David testified that the first vehicle he saw was a big boat of a car, something he could easily say, even under oath, was a muscle car. More laughter erupted from the gallery.

The judge raised his hand to quiet the low but distracting giggles, instantly bringing order back to the courtroom.

David cleared his throat and nodded at the judge's silent warning before continuing. The second vehicle, behind the car, was a van that appeared to be white. When David turned his headlights back on, the other vehicles did the same, momentarily blinding him and then obscuring his view.

With the rules of the road still fresh in his mind from the many hours he spent studying for his driver's test, he knew the car had the right of way. So, he waited. After a few minutes, with a few choice words—he would rather not repeat in the courtroom—he slammed on the gas pedal and headed back to town. After driving a kilometre, he checked his rearview mirror and saw that the car was now following closely behind him. The van had fallen back out of sight. As he watched, he shook his head, as the car suddenly sped up and passed him on the shoulder instead of on the left side of the road—which was clear from any oncoming traffic. This took David by surprise, making him lean forward to peer past Louie to get a "good look" at the stupid idiot behind the wheel.

It was a couple of days later—after he had heard about Kerrie's body being discovered near the stables— that David first contacted the RCMP. He didn't know Kerrie personally, but he had only seen her around the neighbourhood as they both grew up in the Eastwood area and had attended the same elementary school. He had also seen her in the halls of the high school. Regardless, he felt compelled to report what he had witnessed that night, giving the lead investigator a description of both vehicles, along with describing the odd traffic encounter on the road when driving back to the city. David was able to provide the colour of the car with some certainty, describing it as light brown or gold, but he could only guess that the van was white, as it had held back and disappeared in his rearview mirror.

It was when Paul Stanley pulled up to his place of work at the Hillcrest Gas Station, also known as Crazy Pete's, to fill up his tank and ask to cash a third-party check, that David put a name to the man he saw that night. Even though it was against company policy, David cashed the third-party check to get the man's name. That was when he made the second call to the RCMP to tell them he now knew the name of the man he had seen coming out of the stable road. The prosecutor asked David if he recognized that man in the courtroom today.

David sat up straight in his chair and pointed at Paul Stanley. "That's the man I saw coming out of the stable road and who passed me on the shoulder the night Kerrie was murdered."

"How sure are you?" the prosecutor asked.

"Almost positive."

"How positive?" the prosecutor asked.

"Ninety per cent positive," David replied confidently.

Paul Stanley continued to sit stiffly in his chair and stare straight ahead, as the entire gallery turned their heads to shoot daggers at him.

When the Crown had no further questions, the judge ordered a brief recess.

A half an hour later, when David once again took his seat on the witness stand and before the judge returned to the courtroom, I watched as the prosecutor approached David and leaned down to whisper something in his ear. He then handed David a large paperclip. David nodded once before taking it, just as the judge re-entered the court room.

Once the court was called back into order, the Prick stood up and re-buttoned his dark grey pin striped suit jacket while he stared down at his legal notepad. "Do you smoke weed, David?" he asked.

"No, sir," David said loud and clear. "It tends to do a number on my stomach."

Paul's lawyer looked up and nodded at David. "Would you describe yourself to be, what some people would say, a car guy?" he asked.

David shook his head. "No, sir. My specialty is more with the genre of heavy metal music."

This ignited a few low chuckles from the gallery.

The judge allowed it.

"So, correctly identifying the year, make, and model of a car would not be one of your areas of expertise, or specialities, using your own words?" he asked, stepping out from behind the defence table. It only took him two long strides to stand in front of the witness stand, almost blocking my view.

"Yes, sir." David sat up straighter.

"What about colours, David? Are you familiar with colours?" the Prick asked.

"Yes," David replied.

"Because when you initially reported seeing the vehicles leaving the stable road, you first told the police that the colour of the car was green, correct?"

"I'm not sure," David said.

The lawyer walked back to the defence table to pick up a file before turning back to address the witness. "Well, reading from your initial interview with the lead investigator and in your own words in your sworn statement, the colour you used to describe the car you saw that night was greenish, not light brown or a gold colour."

"It's been months since I gave that statement," David admitted.

"Would you like a few minutes to review your sworn statement to help refresh your memory?" the Prick asked politely.

"No. I believe you," David replied.

He dropped the file back on the table. "So, you couldn't identify the year, make or model of the car, and you're not sure of the colour of the car you saw either?"

David shook his head. "I was never sure of the colour of the car; I told the cops that. It looked green, but it was dark, and the fluorescent yellow lights on the Burntwood bridge could have easily distorted the actual colour of the car."

"I see." The Prick nodded. "So, when did you realize you were wrong about the colour?"

"When Paul pulled up at Hillcrest a couple of days later," David said.

"So, you were only sure of the colour of the car when my client pulled up to your place of work?"

"Yes, sir." David shifted in his seat.

For the next hour, the defence attorney hammered David with questions. He asked him over and over how he could be ninety per cent sure it was Paul Stanley that he saw that night, if he couldn't be sure about something as simple as the colour of the car.

David held his own, answering each question hurled at him in a steady, even voice while his fingers fiddled with the paperclip.

I was impressed by David's unwavering testimony and his clear and steady voice. I suddenly realized what the paperclip was for—to keep his hands busy while he was under cross examination and stop David from losing his cool. If it had been me, I would have lost it on the confusion over the colour of the car alone.

Paul Stanley's lawyer wasn't just good; he was better than good. He continued to jump back and forth between questions, from the colour of the car to David's inability to identify the year, make, or model. He then asked how David could, in good conscience, state in this courtroom today that he was almost positive it was Paul Stanley he saw leaving the stable road that night, when he couldn't even be sure of something as simple as the colour of the car. The lawyer, at one point, even implied David may have smoked a little weed that evening—"maybe just one puff?"

How could David have gotten a good look at the driver from the driver's seat, while also having to keep his eye on the road during this odd, and very disturbing passing manoeuvre, he had testified to earlier, when the light brown, gold or greenish car had passed him on the passenger side? How much time would you say it takes to pass a car, David? What was the colour of the car under those fluorescent lights that illuminated the Burntwood bridge again? How could you be ninety per cent sure that the man you saw in a matter of a few seconds was, in fact, Paul Stanley?

It was like watching a verbal tennis match, with the defence attorney hitting hard and fast questions at him and with David hitting right back with clear and steady answers. The clerk stenographer's jaw moved nonstop. The funnel never left her face during the entire cross examination, causing red marks to form on both her cheeks.

"Let's be honest, Mr. Samson, can you testify in this courtroom today with any degree of certainty that it was, in fact, my client that you saw that night?" the Prick asked for the umpteenth time, raising both hands in the air.

"As I have said many times, but I'll say it again, I'm ninety per cent sure it was Paul Stanley I saw the night Kerrie was murdered!" David's patience had run out, his voice now raised as he leaned forward in his seat, as if he was going to jump over the top of the wooden box to tackle the attorney. "What I am one hundred per cent sure of in this courtroom today, sir, is that you are trying to trip me up on my own words to confuse me!"

A sudden eruption of applause exploded from the gallery.

The judge turned swiftly in his chair and slammed his gavel down hard and loud. "Order!" He glared out at the crowded gallery. "There will be no more outburst of any kind or applause in my courtroom."

The courtroom fell silent under the judge's stern gaze.

David's cheeks were now flushed pink. The paperclip out of sight, clenched in his fist.

The defence attorney stood for a moment staring back at the witness, saying nothing, letting the silence in the courtroom build.

David leaned back in his chair, his shoulders relaxing a little.

Finally, Paul's lawyer responded to David's accusation that still hung heavy in the air. "No, Mr. Samson, what I am trying to do here today in this courtroom is establish reasonable doubt." He then turned on the heel of his shiny dress shoe and returned to his seat. "I have nothing further for this witness, your honour."

David's buddy, Louie Longhorn, was called to the stand next, and unlike David's hours on the witness stand, Louie's testimony lasted all of thirty minutes. His voice was low, with a tone of uncertainty with every answer he gave. Even though Louie would have had the best, unobstructed view of the driver of the vehicle that passed them that night, the defence attorney began his cross-examination by pointing out what the Crown had already established, Louie had been high on weed that night. So, no, he could not positively identify the man or the car that had passed them on the wrong side of the road.

Right after David's and Louie's testimony, the Crown's last witness was a middle-aged local man who testified in a gruff voice that he had seen Paul

Stanley cleaning out his car the day after the murder—all afternoon. The witness stated that on that particular Friday, he had made several trips to the city dump while cleaning out his backyard and noticed, with each trip, that Paul wasn't just washing the exterior of his car but was scrubbing the interior as well, which he thought was a bit strange. In his opinion, the car was nothing special—certainly not special enough to warrant the amount of attention Paul was giving it. The car was old and even rusted out in some places.

With no questions from the Prick, the Crown rested its case.

To me, a fourteen-year-old girl who had no legal expertise or experience with the law whatsoever, the Crown's case against Paul Stanley seemed "iffy" at best. Every physical piece of evidence presented during the hearing had a thick layer of doubt covering it.

After supper one night, I went to the bookshelf in the hallway where my father had proudly purchased a complete set of Britanica encyclopedias to find the definition of circumstantial evidence. The definition read: "Evidence pointing indirectly toward someone's guilt but not conclusively proving it." I slammed the heavy book shut, thinking to myself that pretty much summed up the Crown's case.

The entire preliminary hearing against Paul Stanley lasted one week. With each passing day, I sat patiently waiting for that one piece of evidence that would prove Paul had killed Kerrie and would merit proceeding to a "real" murder trial. But there was nothing, nothing that could link Paul to either Kerrie or the crime scene. There was no evidence to show that Paul even *knew* who Kerrie was. The blood stain found in his car turned out to be tomato juice. The two hairs that may have been Kerrie's could not be proven to be hers because there was no forensic test available.

Paul Stanley's lawyer only called witnesses to testify to the whereabouts of his client the night of Kerrie's murder. That night, Paul Stanley shopped for furniture at several stores with a girl friend, before stopping for a beer at the Burntwood Hotel, then for another beer at the Headframe, before going home around 11:00 p.m. to make his lunch for school the next day. He had just started a pre-employment industrial mechanic's course at the local college. His mother swore that Paul was at home during the time the murder took place.

At the end of the proceedings, the judge had no other choice but to stay the charges against Paul Stanley for the murder of Kerrie Ann Brown. There just wasn't enough evidence presented by the provincial Crown prosecutor to warrant moving forward to a murder trial.

During the judge's final statement following his ruling, he addressed the entire courtroom to make clear his decision, explaining that a stay of charges did not mean "not guilty." It just meant there wasn't enough sufficient evidence presented by the Crown prosecution to warrant moving forward to a trial at this point.

The judge said that the two hairs found in the accused's car, which may have been consistent with the victim's hair, were, in fact, under the law, considered to be circumstantial evidence within this evidentiary proceeding. Unlike fingerprints, the science behind testing hair follicles to match them to a victim or a perpetrator was currently nonexistent. However, with advancing technology and testing procedures, retesting the hairs could and would be done in the future.

Emotionally exhausted and physically deflated, we all retreated once again to Dan's basement to recap the week's events and the judge's ruling. Everyone had mixed reactions to the verdict. Some of us were convinced it was Paul Stanley, while others believed the RCMP had jumped the gun, or had tunnel vision, and that Paul was innocent. Some thought that even if he didn't commit the murder, he must have been there that night and possibly knew who did. After all, why would the police focus on him in the first place?

By the end of that lengthy and deep discussion in the basement on Trout Ave, the one thing we all could agree on was that Kerrie's killers were still out there.

CHAPTER 10
NEAR MISS

On the following Sunday, after the preliminary hearing, four cars packed with kids and coolers set off down the highway for the forty-five-minute drive south. There were ten of us venturing out into the great white northern wilderness to spend the day picking purple pinecones under a dark grey sky.

With the fire lit and roaring in the middle of the clearing, the girls carved out their seats in the surrounding snowbank, claiming their spots with their butt imprints. It wasn't long before the pinecone picking production area was in full swing.

A couple of hours later, it became obvious to everyone that we had picked the clearing clean.

"How about I drive up the road to see if there is another clearing like this one?" Ron offered, rubbing his bare hands together over the fire.

With no sun to beat down on us, it was bitterly cold with a slight wind chill, the temperature easily dipping into the minus twenties.

"I'll come with you." Shawna jumped up, slapping the snow from her butt with both hands.

Shawna and I had known each other since elementary school. In the last couple of weeks, she had begun to hang out with us on a regular basis, because she had started to date Ron. She was a slim girl with a bubbly personality with shoulder-length white-blond hair that matched her pale features. When she smiled, she would scrunch up her entire face, which made the dimples deepen on both her cheeks.

"Sounds good," Bruce agreed.

"Bruce, can you grab my heavier mitts from your car?" Rebecca asked, smiling sweetly up at him.

It was also becoming obvious that Rebecca and Bruce were in the beginning stages of their own blossoming relationship.

"Sure, no problem." He smiled down at her, while putting on his skidoo mitts, before turning to follow Ron and Shawna back to the road.

Minutes later, a car engine revved, the loud noise echoed off the surrounding trees and throughout the clearing. Everyone who had gathered around the fire to warm up stopped what they were doing to turn in the direction of the sound.

Dan, who was bent down on one knee, roasting a hot dog at the end of a long stick, stood up to get a better look. "Looks like Bruce got the front end of his car stuck," he said, spearing the stick into a snowbank. The half cooked hot dog now dangled from the other end, helpless. He bent down to pick up his heavy mitts.

"Stuck?" I wrenched my neck sideways to see for myself.

Sure enough, the front end of Bruce's car was off the road and sat at an odd angle with the front of the car pointing into the steep ditch.

As Dan, Geno, and I made our way through the knee-deep snow, Bruce shifted the small sports car into reverse, then into drive, then back into reverse trying to rock the car to coax it onto road, but all he ended up doing was making the front tires spin, digging them deeper into the snow. When we climbed onto the road, Bruce got out of the car and held up both hands in defeat.

"I thought I would warm it up a bit while turning it around now, instead of when we were all leaving and it just slid off the road somehow." He shook his head at his car, with its front end buried deep in the snowbank.

"Okay, get in and we'll try to push you out," Dan said, glancing over at Geno and me.

We both nodded.

As Bruce got back into his car, Natalie and Rebecca crawled up onto the road to join us.

"Man, he's really stuck," Natalie said.

"Ya think?" Rebecca replied sarcastically, smiling at her.

All of us carefully climbed down into the ditch and positioned ourselves around the front of Bruce's car, placing our hands on the hood, getting ready to push. Geno, of course, stood front and centre. He bent down to get a good hold of the bottom of the bumper.

"READY?" Dan shouted.

Bruce nodded through the windshield, then put the car in reverse.

"GIVE 'ER!" Dan yelled.

Bruce stepped on the gas. We never got the chance to push because the front tires spun so fast that it made the white powder shoot straight up into the air, surrounding all of us in a thick cloud of snow.

"STOP!" Dan yelled.

We all stood back, madly blinking the snow from our eyes. I glanced over at Rebecca and burst out laughing. She was covered in the fluffy white powder, her jet-black hair misted white with matching eyelashes.

She wiped her snow-covered face with her bare hand. "Thanks a lot, Bruce!" She laughed out loud.

Bruce jumped out of the car. "Sorry about that, guys!" he said, only his sincere apology didn't match the wide grin on his face. All of a sudden, his head jerked sideways and up to stare at something that had caught his attention. The smile on his face quickly vanished as his mouth fell open.

All of us turned to see what he was looking at.

I stood frozen as the world around me became deadly quiet. When the clock moved forward again, everything I saw appeared to be moving in slow motion. Ron's car had just come over the top of that steep hill and was headed straight for us. At first, the car appeared to be going slow, almost at a crawling pace but then it jerked forward and picked up speed. I gasped when the car took a sharp turn, causing the tires to lose their grip on the icy road.

The car violently swerved left, then right, before skidding to the left again and then veered off the road completely. I watched in horror as the car flew through the air before it crashed into the trees, making a sharp and loud crunching noise. The car had landed with its front end wedged between two tall spruce trees. The back end dropped with a loud bang, then settled on the snow-covered ground which left the front end, pointing straight up towards the dark grey sky.

"OH MY GOD!" Rebecca screamed.

The sound of Rebecca's voice sprang us into action all at once, like a gun going off at the beginning of a race. Without thinking, I crawled out of the ditch and ran at full speed up the steep, icy road. With every second step, my feet slipped on the icy surface, slowing me down. I kept having to readjust my footing to keep myself from falling and rolling back down the hill.

When we reached the spot on the road where the car had gone off, we stood panting, trying to catch our breath as we watched Ron get out of the passenger side of the car. He promptly sunk into the snowbank up to his waist. He cautiously walked behind the car to stand below the open driver's side door. He raised his arms, getting ready to catch Shawna. It took her a few minutes to gather enough courage to jump down into his outstretched arms.

I stood overcome with relief when it became obvious that neither one of them was seriously hurt. They made their way through the waist-deep snow towards us. Once they had climbed safely back onto the road, Shawna's knees buckled, which forced her to sit down hard on her bum. She pulled her knees up to her chest and hugged them and started to cry hysterically.

I knelt down beside her, wrapping my arms around her. "Shh, it's okay. You're okay," I said, my cheek becoming wet from her snow-covered hair.

"I'm so sorry!" she sobbed.

"What the hell happened?" Dan asked Ron.

Ron's face was white as the snow he had just swam through. He shook his head, raised his gloved hands in the air. "She wanted to drive," he replied meekly.

"Seriously!?" Geno barked at him. "You decide to teach your fifteen-year-old girlfriend how to drive on an icy road in the bush out in the middle of fucking nowhere!?"

"Cool it, Geno!" Bruce yelled, shooting Geno a look that said, "You're not helping."

"She panicked. We both did," Ron said, ignoring Geno's glare. "When we came over the top of the hill and saw everyone standing around at the bottom, we both freaked out. She hit the gas instead of the brake, then lost control of the car." He walked over to Shawna and knelt in front of her, patting one of her shoulders awkwardly. "It's okay, Shawna. Seriously, it's no big deal. It's only a car. We're okay, that's all that matters."

"It's no big deal..." Geno mimicked Ron perfectly.

"I didn't want to hit anyone!" Shawna glared up at Geno with tears streaming down her cheeks, then shouted, "The road was just too icy!"

"Well, I'll give you that. You didn't hit anyone," Geno snapped back at her.

Ron stood up and took a step towards Geno.

"UH GUYS!" Brad's sharp, loud voice cut through the tension escalating between Geno and Ron. "I think we're royally screwed," he announced, matter-of-factly.

We all turned at the same time as he climbed out of the ditch and back onto the road. Nobody had noticed that Brad had gone ahead to check out the scene of the accident and investigate how bad the damage was.

"There is no way we're going to get the car out from between those two trees, let alone drag it back onto the road. Unless everyone is okay with it crashing down on top of one of us." He clapped his skidoo mitts together to shake off the snow.

Nobody said a word as the reality of our situation sunk in.

Shawna's hysterical crying had stopped, only now her teeth were chattering, and she was shivering.

"I think she might be in shock," I said to everyone.

"Help her down the hill and get her by the fire to warm up," Dan ordered. "The guys will get Bruce's car unstuck while the girls pack up our things. We should be able to get all of us into three vehicles to drive back to town."

I stood up, pulling Shawna with me. Natalie moved to the other side of her and looped her arm through hers. We held her steady as we cautiously made our way back down the hill.

"And, Ron, if anyone asks, you were the one who was driving," Dan said sharply.

"I know." Ron nodded.

While the guys pushed Bruce's car out of the ditch and back onto the road, the girls packed everything up. Everyone helped load up the three remaining vehicles. An hour later, we were on the highway heading back to town.

Ron and Shawna squeezed into the backseat of Dan's car with Tammy. Shawna's head rested on Ron's shoulder, her cheeks still a bright shade of pink and her eyes still puffy. She was oddly calm—too calm, in fact. She had finally quit apologizing to everyone.

Jade sat in the front seat with me, squishing me in the middle as we rode in an exhausted silence. I leaned my head on Dan's shoulder and stared out at the passing scenery. It had been a long, grey day, and now it was snowing. Large snowflakes were falling fast and furious, dusting the dark green spruce and pine trees that lined the highway. The picture-perfect northern wilderness scene deserved to be captured and preserved on a Christmas card. After a while, my eyelids became heavy, and I was finding it hard to stay awake, either from the hours of fresh air or the trauma I still felt from witnessing the accident.

When my eyes fluttered and then closed, the footage of Ron's car flying through the air would replay in my head, ending with that loud crunching sound as the car's front end jammed itself between the two large spruce trees. I jolted myself awake. Dan took my hand and squeezed it. The expression on his face matched my own. Thank God no one had gotten hurt, or worse, killed. We were lucky, damn lucky. Attending one funeral for a friend was enough to last all of us for a lifetime.

After everyone was safely dropped off at home, both Dan and Bruce offered to go with Ron to tell his parents the bad news about the family's vehicle.

The next day, Dan and Bruce went with Ron and his dad to drive back out to Joey Lake with a tow truck following close behind to rescue the McKenzie's only means of transportation—the car left dangling between two spruce trees in the northern Manitoba forest.

When Ron's dad was first told about the accident, he was furious at his son's carelessness and, within his angry response, questioned his son's level of intelligence. But once Mr. McKenzie saw the car for himself, his anger quickly disappeared, replaced with utter disbelief at what he was seeing, followed by his obvious relief that his son was okay.

While all of them stood at the bottom of that very steep hill staring up, Mr. McKenzie took his toque off to rub his bald head with one hand, then said out loud what everyone was thinking. "You kids are just goddamn lucky no one was killed."

It took the entire day to free the car, and not with one tow truck but two, the second truck dispatched once the tow truck driver and Mr. McKenzie came up with a solid recovery plan. By mid-day, both the rigs had positioned themselves halfway up the hill. Together they managed to pull the car loose from the trees before dragging the car back onto the road just as the sun was setting.

Word about the near-miss accident quickly spread among the parents of the YFBT members. As details about our misadventure were shared, it ignited a heated debate amongst the parents. Some of them demanded to know whose brilliant idea it was in the first place to allow their unsupervised teenagers to go out into the wilderness in below-freezing temperatures to harvest the purple pinecones all on their own.

An informal vote was cast with no second motion required from the leadership of Youth for a Better Tomorrow. The final tally was in favour of kiboshing any of us from taking future trips down the narrow, poorly maintained Joey Lake Road. This abruptly ended our purple pinecone picking adventures, for good.

As the shock of the accident wore off in the weeks that followed, YFBT's fundraising activities slowed down. Full jars with donations continued to be collected from local businesses around town, along with many organizations who also continued to donate money, which kept the scholarship fund's bank account growing at a steady pace.

At the end of May, Tom stood up, either ignoring or forgetting about the microphone in front of him to announce that Youth for a Better Tomorrow had reached its goal of raising ten thousand dollars, along with some pocket change.

The city council chambers erupted into applause.

With the money raised to establish The Kerrie Ann Brown Memorial Scholarship Fund, Youth for a Better Tomorrow's final goal was achieved. We voted in favour of using the left-over money to purchase a large plaque to record the names of future recipients below Kerrie's picture, which we hoped would memorialize Kerrie—forever.

***

The best thing about who we all were before that god-awful October night was that we had lived, for a time, being carefree, goofy, adventurous teenagers. All of us, with our combined youthful ignorance, hadn't the slightest idea something bad could ever happen to us. We were happy, bonded by our immaturity and incapable of recognizing possible risks, seeing potential hazards or identifying eminent dangers that might lie ahead—like one of us getting on the hood of a car in bare feet to surf through a narrow branch covered road, or running around stopped cars at a red light to tag another car "it" or guzzling a beer, or even, just lighting a cigarette. Within our oblivious, blissful teenage existence, we only saw good instead of evil, more blue sky than storm clouds. We lived only in our todays without ever thinking about our tomorrows. That is until Kerrie was taken away from us.

In June, when Bruce, Dan and I took centre stage at the Letkemann Theatre to present the very first Kerrie Ann Brown Memorial Scholarship, I took a small step backwards into the shadows and out of the spotlight. Bruce spoke first about Kerrie and the overwhelming support Youth for a Better Tomorrow had received from the community with helping us reach our goal. I felt proud, with a sense of accomplishment at what we had done together for Kerrie, but I couldn't shake off this underling feeling of sadness that came over me the minute I got on that stage.

I shook my head when Dan tried to pull me forward, to stand beside him. He then gently squeezed my hand before letting it go and stepped forward, by himself, up to the microphone to announce the name of the graduate with the highest mark in English.

As I stood in the shadows alone, I scanned the familiar faces of the first two rows in the packed auditorium. The Brown family sat front and centre, surrounded by all of Kerrie's friends, each one of them wearing matching smiles. When the entire theatre stood up to clap, to cheer, to hoot and to holler, I followed their lead by clapping while forcing a smile.

The bittersweet explosion of applause was amplified by this nagging feeling of sorrow. It felt like we had reached the end of "something." I just couldn't put my finger on what that "something" *was*.

It was when Dan, Bruce and I left the stage together to go find our separate seats within the dark theatre that I finally pinpointed exactly what I was feeling and why I was feeling it. It was inevitable, just a part of life's grand plan, that at some point, more specifically this point in time, all of us were going to grow up and move on with our lives—something Kerrie Ann Brown would never do.

***

Youth for a Better Tomorrow had no real chance of surviving past awarding the first Kerrie Ann Brown memorial scholarship in June 1987. With a handful of its members graduating in the spring of 1987 and with no succession plan in place, the streetwise group would eventually dissolve as the founding members grew up and moved on with their lives.

The only evidence of Youth for a Better Tomorrow's existence is the memorial plaque with Kerrie's smiling face on it, which hangs in the library at RD Parker high school today.

CHAPTER 11
WHAT I KNOW NOW

Almost four decades later...

How do you write the ending to a story that has no end, when the characters' faces slowly fade away while the plot thins? Letting those loose threads flap aimlessly in the literary wind while searching for the words to write on that last blank page.

Our story reminds me of those movies or television series where the TV screen suddenly turns to black, making you snatch the remote and madly push every button. Only to realize the abrupt ending to the story was part of the grand plan, being strategically creative in leaving it up to the viewer to decide the characters' fate and the plot's conclusion. From the beginning, *The Deafening Sound of Sorrow* never really had an ending. The book's sole purpose was to change the narrative surrounding Kerrie, focusing more on her and her friends than on the unsolved murder. Our story, with no ending, might ignite feelings of frustration, helplessness, or injustice of some sort. Ironically, that is how Kerrie's loved ones have felt since October 18th, 1986, when her body was discovered in the woods north of the city.

Because I did not attend Dan's party and bear witness to what happened that fateful night, I could not, in good conscious, extend a straight pointed finger at any viable suspects. In retrospect, it was a small blessing for me to have been in Flin Flon that weekend, because I would never have to experience, over the next four decades, that unexpected call from an RCMP officer, or a newly assigned investigator, in Kerrie's case. That decaying clawed hand reaching out from the past to grab hold and try to shake out fresh memories or possible new information. Forcing witnesses to rehash the fall of 1986 to remember, to recount, and to go over the events of that night, over and over again.

It wasn't just Chris' unexpected phone call that lit a writer's spark in me to write our never-ending story. It was Mr. David Ridgen and his CBC true crime podcast, *Somebody Knows Something*, that hurled me back in time. To find myself, once again, submerged in that black abyss of shock, grief, and anger and to be reminded of the gruesome details of Kerrie's last moments on earth.

Mr. Ridgen's podcast was well done. He took his time with thoroughly reporting the details of the cold case which captivated his listening audience. He didn't just interview witnesses and follow up on old leads, he also explored and exposed rumours. Rumours that had whispered in the shadows in the back of my mind of potential suspects over the years.

Robert Delaronde was one of those suspects. If only because not long after Kerrie's murder, he hung himself. Which left behind a cloud of suspicion about his possible involvement. When his sister spoke of his struggles with bi-polar disorder in the podcast, the erratic behaviour I had witnessed and the rumours that had swirled around him took a turn from suspicion to sympathy.

I remember vividly, one day after school, I went to meet Dan and found myself unwittingly joining a group of kids who had gathered in the forum to hear a male voice shouting out. Once immersed in the crowd, I stood on my tippy toes and stretched my neck to see Robert. He was standing in the middle and at the bottom of the circle. I watched, impressed both by his bigger-than-life presence and how he had captured the attention of what appeared to be the entire high school. I strained my ears to listen to him but didn't understand a word he said. He made no sense. He babbled on about this and that, talking about the rights of students and how the school had no authority.

When our principal stepped out and in front of the growing student body to call out his name, a silence fell over the crowd. "ROBERT! Would you come and talk to me? Please step into my office." The principal raised one hand to summon him in a stern and steady voice. He wore his usual loose fitting business suit over his short round frame, his thinning black hair cut short and styled to show off his middle age. He knew very well—as we all did—that he was no match for Robert Delaronde, who was built like a brick shithouse, standing over six-feet-tall, and with broad shoulders that stretched into his thick biceps.

Robert made a sudden move towards a three-sided, chest-high booth used to sell tickets for student raffles or the latest student theatre production in the Letkemann Theatre. Using only one muscular arm, he dragged the wooden booth into the middle of the forum, with little effort, and in record time, before turning to face the principal. "HOW ABOUT YOU STEP INTO MY FUCKING OFFICE!" he yelled. This was followed by a thundering roar of applause from mostly all who were watching. Our principal turned on the heels of his black dress shoes and headed back to his office, leaving Robert with his pumped-out chest to babble on.

When the principal reappeared, he ordered all the students and a few teachers who had gathered to leave now, informing us that the RCMP had been called. I learned later it would take two officers to wrestle Robert to the ground and drag him out of the school, never to return again. When Dan and I got into his car to go home, I remember saying to him it would have been awesome if only he had a point to his speech, but Robert appeared confused and sounded delirious.

Because of the podcast, I learned that instead of drug abuse or living with guilt, Robert lived his last days in a time when little was known about or help offered to people living with bi-polar disorder. Which left Robert to battle his mental illness all on his own. It now seemed plausible that he had succumbed to the demons that raged inside his head when choosing to take his own life.

With this revelation, I have tried to coach myself in recent years to quit playing the guessing game of Who-Done-It. I've stopped myself from studying those old photographs with the faces of all the teenage boys I hung out with long ago to search for some shimmering outline of guilt in their young features or hideous secret hidden behind their eyes. While listening to the podcast with my headphones on, I stopped dusting a bookshelf in my living room, when David Ridgen's made-for-radio voice asked my ex-boyfriend if it was possible that someone at the party that night could have done it. I held my breath. "...how could you do something like that and live amongst us? So that gets me to 'no,' I don't think. I don't believe, not for a second, that it was anybody with us that night." I exhaled my agreement. In my heart, I too believed that. Whoever raped and bludgeoned Kerrie to death couldn't have known her, been friends with her, or dated her. It would mean they would have known the girl she was and what she meant to so many. They could not have known her. Because if they had, they would not have done what they did to her and be able to still walk among us.

In 1987, the physical evidence presented by the Crown prosecution during the preliminary hearing included a coarse black hair, two blond hairs that were "consistent" with Kerrie's but not a definitive match, and a red stain discovered in Paul Stanley's car that, after testing, proved to be a tomato-based juice. In the late 1990s, with the emergence of DNA forensic science, the RCMP began a country-wide campaign testing potential suspects, which brought a renewed sense of hope to the cold case. Around this time, the RCMP also made public other evidence collected near or at the crime scene: a square floor mat and a red and blue air mattress. Where they were found suggested that one of the monster's vehicles had become stuck in the mud, and these items were used to free it. The most unsettling and disturbing piece of evidence disclosed to the public at this time was that there wasn't just one semen sample recovered, but two separate samples. This meant two different monsters had sexually assaulted her. Unbelievably, this new information painted an even more nightmarish picture of Kerrie's last hours.

The problem when remembering Kerrie is my mind cannot help but take that sharp turn to imagine how she died. The violence she tried so hard to fend off, the rapes she endured, the utter brutality of it all. Then for her to be left out in the cold for hours, to die alone, under a dark October night sky. It was so hard to listen to and try to absorb Bob Urbanoski's interview in the podcast, a subject-matter-expert in victimology. He recalled his theories of the perpetrators, who he believed had to have known the spot where Kerrie was found. How could they not? The stable road was off a main highway, well hidden, and right out of place. The murder weapons they used, tree branches, logs, and sticks, showed that her killers didn't start out the night with the intent of killing, as they had to make do with whatever they could gather from the surrounding forest. Evidence found at the scene and on her body proved a frenzied and spontaneous attack, suggesting inexperience, not knowing how many blows it would take, so they just kept on hitting. Mr. Urbanoski's interview would leave me shaken by the graphic images he conjured up, stuck for some time in that dark abyss, with these thoughts in my head that played on repeat. How is it humanly possible for anyone to do what they did to her and still carry on with their lives? To get married? To have a family? To have a daughter of their own? My fucking god, what they did to Kerrie and how she had suffered.

As to Mr. Ridgen's comparison of Kerrie's murder to the Helen Betty Osborne case, a young Aboriginal girl brutally murdered by three white men in The Pas Manitoba in 1971, I have mixed feelings. Yes, there are similarities between the two murder cases. Both involved teenage girls who were snatched on their way home to be brutally murdered and left out in the cold, with one distinct glaring difference between them—Helen Betty's case was eventually solved where Kerrie's case has not. Whether one girl was white or one girl was Aboriginal, to me, is absolutely irrelevant. I refuse to focus on the racial aspects of each case when comparing the murders of both girls. Black, brown, white or yellow, they both, separately, were made to endure their own brutally violent death at the hands of monsters who showed them no mercy. The colour of their skin means nothing. Both girls were innocent and undeserving of the fate handed down to them, which left behind the same echoing sound of sorrow to the people who knew and loved them the most.

Today, I know as much as a Google search can tell me about the status of Kerrie's murder investigation. Your guess is as good as mine as to where her cold case stands. What about all the evidence that was collected? The fourteen thousand records, all contained in forty-five bankers' boxes, filled with forensic evidence, witness statements, the floor mat, the air mattress, and those valuable DNA samples. What about it? When a constable with the D Division Historical Case Unit in Winnipeg, Manitoba, reluctantly spoke to the CBC reporter, I was immediately put off by her tone of self-importance and unwarranted confidence, which bordered on arrogance—I suspect a common personality trait among most seasoned RCMP officers. Within her carefully scripted answers, she had an air about her which reeked of defensive indignation in every answer given. Instead of a more fitting professional embarrassment. It is human nature to want to point blame when something bad and unexpected happens. As the cold case stands now, unsolved and with Kerrie's monsters remaining faceless and free. I find it relatively easy to point some of the blame at the head/general investigator, the lead investigator, the RCMP officers, the media liaisons, public relations officers, and all the cold case investigators who have been involved with Kerrie's murder case back then and now.

Kerrie's murder slowly and systematically destroyed her own family. Her mother, Ann Brown, passed away fifteen years after her daughter's horrific death, losing her battle with cancer. Which left her husband to grieve in the house Kerrie grew up in until his own passing in the fall of 2023. In the decades that followed, Jim Brown remained steadfast in the past, angry, trying to seek out his daughter's killers, never moving forward or away from the family home. Kerrie's two older brothers would live their own lives battling separate but equally brutal wars with addiction and mental illness. The Brown family never got over Kerrie's death. Ultimately, succumbing to that black abyss of shock, grief, and anger.

Natalie and Rebecca were both interviewed separately by the CBC's true crime reporter. When hearing their voices again after so many years, it tugged at my heartstrings. They sounded good. They sounded strong. But it was something in Natalie's voice that made me stop cleaning and sit down on my couch to lean forward and listen intently to her words. The cloak of guilt was still heavy on her shoulders. It was evident in her voice, even after all these years. It broke my heart to think about her having to carry that burden throughout her life, and the strength it took. Natalie would remain forever stuck in my mind as one of the bravest teenage girls I had ever known, a true survivor. Both girls' families had packed up their daughters within the year or two following their best friend's murder, to physically remove them from the geographical reminders of the tragedy and to help both girls heal and move on with their lives. However hard Youth for a Better Tomorrow tried, Thompson Manitoba was never the same again. The streets no longer felt safe, and the surrounding thick boreal forest now appeared ominous. One of the coldest murder cases in Manitoba's history still hovers like a dark cloud over the northern city.

As to the burning question of whatever happened to so and so. I have to admit; I lost touch with all of them. I left my hometown, at seventeen years old, to forge ahead in my own life. Over the years, I have secretly stalked some of them, peeking in on their social media accounts to check in on them to see how they were doing. Usually, when their older but so familiar faces would pop up within the platform asking if I knew this person. I knew them once. Not anymore.

Bruce, Geno, Buddy, Tammy, Dan, all of them, the original youth with hopes of a better tomorrow, are long gone, and are now adults. Even Chris Jones, shortly after that unexpected phone call, once again faded away to sink back into that shallow pool of my past. Whatever life path they chose, whatever trials and tribulations they faced and overcame in the years since, it is their story that only they alone can tell. My intention for this book was never to delve into their personal lives, or to be that cold decaying hand reaching out from the past to scratch open wounds that have long since scarred over. Wherever their lives took them and whatever became of them, I hope and pray that they are living well and at peace within their own tomorrows.

In 2010, my husband and I went to the movies to watch the newly released *Lovely Bones*. My husband had picked the movie for our weekly date night, believing I would enjoy it. I didn't. It was a fictional story about a young, innocent teenage girl brutally murdered by a serial monster. Near the end, she was given the choice to either kiss a boy or reveal her killer—she chose to kiss the boy. When I stood to button up my winter coat, it was then and there I decided I hated true crime dramas. The storyline was a harsh reminder that there were real monsters living hidden in this world who were capable of committing horrendous acts against innocent children. When the lights came on in the theatre, it was the very first time the thought ever crossed my mind that Kerrie's monsters may never be caught. That thought, coupled with the lingering sadness from that depressing movie, would once again ignite the deep-seated anger I felt towards Kerrie's killers, a stark reminder of how profoundly unfair life could be.

What I know now, after writing this book, is that I never really *knew* Kerrie Ann Brown and, sadly, neither will you. The few memories I do have of her—those quick, brief snippets of time that have popped up unexpectedly and without warning over the years—have ultimately taught me that if there was any point of Kerrie's short life and violent, brutal death was that there's no excuse to waste any time on this earth; if anything, her murder was more reason to embrace life.

And, in the end, whether Kerrie's murder remains unsolved or not, it will never change the fact that every fall on that dreaded anniversary date those who knew her, however briefly, will forever be connected by time—within the passing hours and minutes of that one day—when we take a moment to remember Kerrie together.

EPILOGUE
...BECAUSE OF KERRIE

Because of Kerrie, at fourteen, I took my very first sip of life's tragic cocktail, composed of equal parts shock, anger, and grief. The frosty cup forced to my lips filled to the brim with life's cruelty that left me gagging and choking with the bitter aftertaste of rape and murder, to purge what little time I had left on the tick ticking clock of my childhood, forcing me to grow up fast with now knowing how truly unfair life could be.

Because of Kerrie, I learned real monsters did not live hidden within the depths of my dark closet or lie in wait in the shadows under my bed. Real monsters lived among us, cleverly dressed in their human disguises, cloaked under the brightness of day. Real monsters had the power to blend in with society while slipping through the fingers of justice to continue to live among us.

Because of Kerrie, I came to realize that the shock, anger, and grief that had festered inside of me over the years by focusing only on my hatred towards her killers, would eventually eat away at my very soul, like a cancer left untreated. It would take me decades to learn how to wrestle her monsters back into the depths of my closet and within the shadows under my bed to turn the light on and shine it where it belonged: on Kerrie and the girl she once was.

Because of Kerrie, I measured my personal net worth by taking stock of the value of each year, month, day, hour, minute, and second that passed during my lifetime. Within my luck of each passing day that I drew from my life's deck, I taught myself to be present within every moment while being an active participant in my life experiences.

Because of Kerrie, shortly after giving birth to my firstborn and feeling his steady pulse beneath my fingertips, my heart burst open with a sudden array of erratic emotions of every shape, size, and colour. As strange and coincidental as life can prove itself to be, my son shared the same birthday as Kerrie. This sudden reminder of my past friend allowed me to fully understand the true value of what I was holding in my arms; the means to measure the pain one feels when losing a child. The emotional impact of that one moment was indescribable, making me hold my newborn son a little tighter.

Because of Kerrie, when my fifteen-year-old daughter, with her hand on her hip and her chin raised upwards fanning a maturity not yet earned, demanded to go to her first party, *Kerrie* suddenly appeared standing beside her. The similarities between them were uncanny. The moment literally took my breath away—both girls were so young, so beautiful, and so innocent. Kerrie's unexpected apparition told me it was time to introduce my old friend to my baby girl. And within that introduction, I shared the details of my fifteen-year-old friend's brief life and brutal death. I hoped that in knowing about Kerrie, at most, it would prevent my daughter's life from ending the same way. And, at the very least, my daughter would never have to drink from the same frosty cocktail that I had too, so many years ago.

Because of Kerrie, I have experienced the time travelling powers of a single song. It does not matter where I am, who I am with, or what I am doing; when "Hotel California" plays the melody catapults me back to sitting on that couch, in that basement on Trout Ave in the summer of 1986, surrounded by all my friends; talking, singing, and laughing. And for reasons that can not be explained, the sound of Kerrie's laughter always rises above us all.

Because of Kerrie, I saw and felt the world deeply. She gave me the gift of insight while teaching me to recognize treasured moments and to cherish the important people in my life. Yet, I always knew, because of her, that at any gifted moment during my lifetime, it could all be easily taken away.

Because of Kerrie Ann Brown, I am and will be forever grateful for the life I was able to live.

ACKNOWLEDGMENTS

This is the step within the publishing process where I am supposed to thank and acknowledge the people who have supported me while writing this book. Naturally, my mind starts to create a mental list. My hardworking "all action and no words" farmer husband who has not read one word I have written in the thirty-four years we have been together, yet has been a constant force standing behind me, pushing me to keep writing when I have, at times, put down my pen. My son, whose bear hugs have kept me sane when the words would not come, who has always been a steady source of comfort when I needed it the most. My beautiful, spirited daughter who would utter the same profane words I did under her breath with every rejection letter I received. My childhood best friend who would squash any doubts about my writing ability with a simple look. All my friends and co-workers who have voiced their concerns that when a literary agent or publisher (Thank you, Black Rose Writing!) finally recognized my God-given talent, I would leave them behind covered in the dust of my fame and fortune. How could I not acknowledge my two favourite cousins, whose cheers would echo in the back of my mind, matching the rhythmic sound of my fingernails clicking on my keyboard? And, finally my, unlikely, longstanding friendship with a certain logical-thinking mechanical engineer who has kept my emotions in check by calmly telling me, "You got this."

These people have supported me by simply urging me to just "keep writing." Yet my heart leads me back to one glaring fact in my life I cannot ignore—just how damn lucky I am. I am very lucky to have so many amazing people in my corner that have lifted me up or pushed me forward when I needed it the most, and not just with my writing. As a woman, wife, mother, friend, and now a published author, I am incredibly grateful for the life I have, surrounded by these amazing people. I can only pray my luck continues.

Today the city of Thompson looks nothing like the town I grew up in. When the nickel mine shut down the refinery and smelting departments in recent years because of environmental regulations, it ultimately affected the northern city by devastating the local economy along with its most vulnerable population *by increasing unemployment, poverty, and crime rates. Yet, I want, or need, to believe my hometown that is still surrounded by that resilient boreal forest and beneath those breathtaking northern lights, there is still hope for a better future. I hold on to that hope that there are youth living within city limits who have the absolute power to change and conquer the challenges the city is facing today, in search of their own better tomorrows.*

This book is dedicated to them, Thompson's youth, because without them there is no chance for any kind of tomorrow.

ABOUT THE AUTHOR

Kathleen Ricard is a wannabe writer of both fiction and nonfiction. Born and raised in Thompson, Manitoba, she discovered her passion for storytelling amid the rugged beauty of the North. She later settled on a small farm in southeast Saskatchewan, where she raised a family and, at last count, over a billion leaf-cutter bees. A self-declared Senior Bee Specialist, she balances farm life with her love of travel, ensuring her handsome husband gets away from the farm at least once a year to relax.

After a *long* career with the provincial government, Kathleen retired to focus on writing. She is the recipient of the 1992 Iona Weenusk Award. *The Deafening Sound of Sorrow* is her debut book.

NOTE FROM KATHLEEN RICARD

Word-of-mouth is crucial for any author to succeed. If you enjoyed *The Deafening Sound of Sorrow*, please leave a review online—anywhere you are able. Even if it's just a sentence or two. It would make all the difference and would be very much appreciated.

Thanks!
Kathy Ricard

We hope you enjoyed reading this title from:

www.blackrosewriting.com

Subscribe to our mailing list – *The Rosevine* – and receive **FREE** books, daily deals, and stay current with news about upcoming releases and our hottest authors.
Scan the QR code below to sign up.

Already a subscriber? Please accept a sincere thank you for being a fan of Black Rose Writing authors.

View other Black Rose Writing titles at www.blackrosewriting.com/books and use promo code **PRINT** to receive a **20% discount** when purchasing.

www.ingramcontent.com/pod-product-compliance
Lightning Source LLC
Chambersburg PA
CBHW072158070526
44585CB00015B/1193